# THE NIBBLER'S DIET™

S.R. Kaura, MD
and
Diane Collins, RD

Manisha press

The Nibbler's Diet™
The Ultimate Solution to America's Weight and Cholesterol Problems.
By S.R. Kaura, MD, and Diane Collins, RD

The Nibbler's Diet™ is a registered trademark.

The information presented in this book has been obtained from authentic and reliable sources. Reprinted material has been printed with permission from the sources given. References are listed. Although great care has been taken to ensure the accuracy of the information presented, the authors and the publisher cannot assume responsibility for the validity of all the materials or the consequences of their use.

Editors: Mary Ellen McLeod and Sarah Whitehouse
Book design and composition by Sans Serif, Inc., Ann Arbor, MI.
Jacket design by B J Graphics, Ypsilanti, MI.
Printing by Edward Bros., Ann Arbor, MI.

ISBN: 0-9650621-0-4

*To all who understand that we are what we make of ourselves through our own dedication and application. Best wishes as you make it happen for yourself.*

# CONTENTS

# PREFACE

As health-care professionals, we have seen many patients caught in a pattern of frustrating, oftentimes unhealthy and usually unsuccessful dieting. We have seen individuals in desperation for a magic cure and quick fix turn to many useless, temporary and expensive programs. Many times patients will lose some or all of their excess weight only to regain their extra pounds—and often more—once they resume their old eating habits. Prompted by many scientific studies and our experiences with our patients, a diet based on nibbling—many small meals—was developed. It has proven to be a very exciting approach to weight loss and has helped many individuals achieve long-term weight loss.

This diet is the result of the collaboration between myself, a family physician, and Diane Collins, RD, a registered dietitian. I have had many years of experience assisting patients with making the life-style changes needed to regain and maintain their health. Diane Collins, RD, brought expertise in nutrition, food choices and the emotional aspects of eating to the project. Together we have piloted a food plan based on many small, satisfying meals. Those who have followed the diet are not hungry, find the selections easy to prepare and maintain and have been able to make lasting changes in their eating habits.

This plan can be successful for you. Overweight patients who have followed this simple program have been able to lose weight, some of them many, many pounds. Slowly and steadily they have been able to reshape their bodies and reach levels of fitness they had not known in many years. Some patients have lost as much as 70 pounds over six months and have kept it off. Many others have lost significant amounts of excess weight. The word has spread about the Nibbler's Diet™. Many patients have followed the program and their friends and relatives have joined the weight-loss effort. We have received calls from across the country from people who have heard of the diet and want more information.

The reasons the Nibbler's Diet™ has become so popular and is so successful are:

- Approximately 10% of the calories in the 1,000-, 1,200- and 1,500-calorie plans are fat calories (about 17% of the calories in the 1,800-calorie diet are from fat). The body needs some fat—around 5% of the caloric intake—to remain healthy. The Nibbler's Diet™ includes sufficient fat so you do not feel deprived.
- It features frequent meals that keep the metabolic rate high. Lowered metabolism is the main problem with many calorie-restricted diets. A diet plan that is very low in calories and does not include exercise can actually lower the metabolic rate.
- An exercise plan complements the diet, further stimulating the metabolism.
- Dieters are not hungry on the plan. Hunger can cause well-intentioned dieters to lose control. With the Nibbler's Diet™ there is no hunger. You eat small meals throughout the day. Most of the patients on the plan say they cannot eat all the food allowed on the diet.
- Dieters lose fat pounds and retain muscle bulk so they maintain their strength and keep up their metabolism.
- Patients say they feel wonderful—energetic and alert—on the Nibbler's Diet™.
- The program is based on self help. There isn't a re-

liance on expensive shakes, powders, prepared and packaged foods or medicines.

- The number of calories can be adjusted for each individual's needs.
- All the difficult barriers presented by other dieting regimes have been overcome so weight reduction is within your grasp. You will find this meal plan easy to follow for the rest of your life.

With best wishes from both of us to all of you.

S.R. Kaura, MD
Diane Collins, RD

Examples of claims of common weight loss products and programs featured in popular magazines. (From *Story M: Adolescent Lifestyle and Eating Behavior*, in Mahan, L. K., and Rees, J.M.; *Nutrition in Adolescence*. St. Louis, CV. Mosby Company, 1984). Printed with permission.

# I

# INTRODUCTION TO OBESITY

## WHY ANOTHER DIET PLAN?

As a nation, Americans are obsessed with obesity, weight loss and health. Up to half of all Americans think they need to lose weight. At any given time 65 million Americans are following some type of diet.[1] Half of all women and one-quarter of all men are trying to lose weight.[2] Many dollars—much of it wasted on ineffective and even dangerous "solutions"—are spent on diet-related programs and services. In 1989, for example, $32 billion were spent in the battle against excess pounds. In the 1990s, our continued obsession with dieting will boost that investment to $51 billion and more.[3]

The overall costs are staggering and individually dieters can spend many hundreds of dollars on what are often ill-advised dieting gimmicks and programs. It is not unusual to find participants in weight-loss programs paying $2,000 for a 12-week program.[4] Individuals can also invest many dollars trying one ineffective approach after another.

At present, the health bill in America is over $650 billion each year. A large portion of this money is spent on

*On his doctor's advice, Bob watches how he eats.*
Printed with permission. Courtesy Mark Heath.

fighting chronic disease related to poor diet and obesity. Cardiovascular disease, hypertension, stroke, cancer, diabetes and gastrointestinal diseases all have a strong link to excess weight. If everyone with medically significant obesity followed a healthy diet like the Nibbler's Diet™, expenditures on health care could be trimmed by 25%. The Centers for Disease Control and Prevention projects there could be a savings of $150 billion annually if Americans would follow a more healthy diet.[5]

Despite the claims made by many commercial programs, the huge investment in time, money and effort and individuals' best intentions, the sad fact is that most plans just don't work. Only 5% of the dieters obtain significant and long-term weight loss. The rest will gain back not only the weight lost but even additional pounds within the next year.[11]

The Nibbler's Diet™ is an excellent and exciting new plan. We know this is probably not the first diet information you have read. Most people who are overweight try many different approaches to losing weight before finding one that works. Most dieting approaches have the seeds of their own failure built into them. They may do any one or more of the following:

*Reduce metabolism*: As individuals diet the body attempts to compensate from the sudden decrease in fuel by reducing metabolism. The body, in effect, becomes very efficient at storing instead of burning the food that it does receive.

*Hunger*: Some diet plans are so skimpy in the volume of food permitted that dieters feel hungry and find it difficult, if not impossible, to stick to the diet. Hunger breaks down the willpower to diet and can lead to binge eating.

*Dissatisfaction*: Some diets attempt to restrict food choices to only a few foods or the foods offered may be very different from those the dieter is used to.

*Depression*: Many plans set dieters up for failure by establishing unrealistic expectations and making dieters feel as if they have failed when they deviate from the plan or don't lose as many pounds as expected. Feelings of worthlessness and failure establish a cycle that most dieters find impossible to break.

*Fitness failure*: Developing muscle is a key to pumping up the metabolism. Diets that focus only on food intake and not on overall fitness may reduce the dietary fat and result in short-term weight losses, but they don't help the dieter develop a healthy and vibrant body.

The Nibbler's Diet™ addresses each of these problems, making weight loss an attainable goal. This is important to know for people going on the Nibbler's Diet™ that weight loss should not be viewed as an all-or-nothing proposition. Even a modest weight loss accomplished sensibly carries many health benefits. A recent study suggested that many of the hazards associated with obesity can be alleviated by even a 10% weight reduction. Modest weight loss, even if an optimal weight is not achieved, is better than none.

# II

# Body Composition and Obesity

## WHAT IS OBESITY?

Obesity develops as individuals accumulate an abnormally large amount of fat. Obesity is defined as 20% or more above desirable weight and this obesity is considered medically significant. There are health risks associated with obesity. A body-fat measurement, the percent of body weight that is composed of fat, is the most accurate measure of a person's obesity level. Adult men are considered obese if they have a body-fat measurement of 25% or greater, and women 30% or greater.[6]

## PREVALENCE OF OBESITY

If you are struggling with a weight problem, you are not alone. The first National Health and Nutrition Examination done in the early 1970s showed almost 29 million Americans were overweight; of these, 8.4 million were severely overweight. A second study completed in 1980 showed the number of overweight individuals had grown

# WHO'S A COUCH POTATO?

Prevalence of sedentary lifestyle by population groups in 1991.

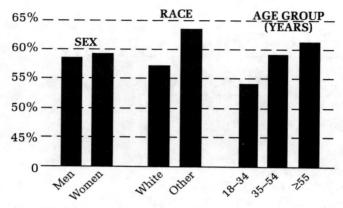

Because of limitations in sample sizes, race-specific prevalences could be estimated only for non-Hispanic whites and other races combined.

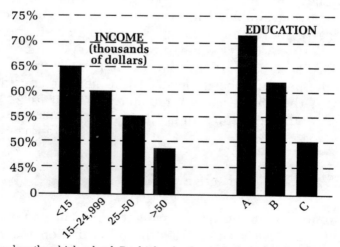

A = less than high school; B = high school or technical school graduate; and C = college attendee or graduate

Courtesy Charles Culhane. Reprinted with permission. Originally appeared in *American Medical News*, August 1993

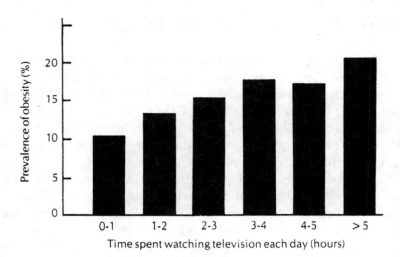

Prevalence of obesity in 12- to 17-year-old adolescents as related to the hours of television viewed daily. Reprinted with permission from *American Family Physician*.

to 34 million. Of these, 13 million were severely overweight. Overweight was defined as 20% above desirable body weight and severely overweight as 40% above desirable body weight.[7]

Sadly the prevalence of obesity in America is increasing. This has been seen in the last four national health surveys that were performed in 1960 to 1962, 1971 to 1974, 1976 to 1980 and 1988 to 1991. In the 1976 to 1980 survey 21.6% were obese. Today that number is 33.4%—one-third of adult Americans![8]

In the United States, obesity tends to increase as people age. Race can also be a factor; a greater percentage of the black population is obese compared to whites.

## WHY ARE AMERICANS GETTING FATTER?

In the past, the causes of obesity were classified into two schools of thought: nature and nurture. Some researchers thought that it was mainly a genetic influence that caused people to become overweight. Others believed the eating patterns established in families contributed to the problem. We now know there are many factors that enter into any individual's tendency to gain weight.

That isn't to say that nature and nurture don't have roles in weight. A number of studies of adopted children have shown a strong relationship between their weight and that of their biological parents and not much relationship between their weight and that of their adoptive parents. It appears that heredity may explain 30–35% of an individual's weight with the rest linked to environmental factors.[9] The genetic role appears to be much stronger in some groups. For example, there is an extraordinarily high obesity rate in Native Americans. Recently a gene has been discovered by researchers which appears to alter the metabolism and prevents the brain from knowing when the stomach is full.

Heredity can make people vulnerable to weight gain, but environmental factors such as the taste and availability of food, eating habits, exercise habits and other life-style choices also influence weight. In North America food is plentiful and palatable with an unusually high reliance on high-calorie, fatty food. Living in these circumstances can make you more vulnerable to developing a weight problem.

In addition, the consumption of alcohol, which is very calorie dense, is very high, particularly among men. This makes up 5–7% of the total calorie intake in the United States.[10] Another factor in weight gain that's seen more often now is the decline of smoking in the last decade. More and more people are quitting smoking. After quitting, people can smell and taste food better and tend to gain weight.

## THE BASIC WEIGHT EQUATION

The basic equation for obesity is an imbalance between the energy intake (the calories we eat) and the energy expenditure (how much we burn as we go about our activities). It is similar to a bank account. If you keep depositing money into your account, you will accumulate a big bank balance. If you withdraw more than you deposit, your checks will begin bouncing. In the human body, a couch potato with little activity and a normal or large intake of food is going to accumulate weight. However, if people are active and "spend" their calories through exercise and their other daily activities, they will be slim.

Calories ingested − calories expended =
weight loss or gain

In general, life has become "too easy" for all of us. Modern appliances, TVs, VCRs, microwaves, automobiles, etc., have helped to reduce our energy expenditure. Soon, robots will start serving breakfast in bed.

The metabolic rate, how efficiently your body uses calories, is related to your lean body mass (LBM) or muscle mass. Young people generally have high metabolisms because they also usually have high lean body mass. Their bodies tend to burn more calories. As we age, the body composition changes so that even if we maintain the same body weight, the ratio of muscle mass to overall weight decreases. As a result, we burn fewer calories. The reason for this is that fats sit in the body while muscles burn calories even when you are sleeping. This sets the stage for the weight gain that many view as a normal part of the aging process.

This is why exercise is such a valuable and essential component of weight loss. Exercise maintains lean body mass, burns calories and increases the metabolic rate.

The metabolic rate is also affected by the timing of when you exercise. If you exercise before eating, more energy is expended in digestion. This phenomenon is more pronounced in persons with higher lean body mass.

A small percentage of individuals may have an underactive thyroid which can decrease the metabolic rate. Although many people would like to blame their thyroid glands, most of us have only our own poor eating and exercise habits to blame.

On the energy intake side of the equation, "we are what we eat" is apt. The type of food consumed as well as the frequency and timing of eating are important. Food has three main components: protein, fat and carbohydrates. Dietary fat is the most notorious component because it is easily converted into body fat. The fat you consume can be taken directly to the fat cell by enzymes. It is more difficult for carbohydrates to be transformed into fat, but if the body is oversupplied with carbohydrates, the glucose in carbohydrates can be converted into fatty acids which can be stored by the fat cells as triglycerides. It is possible but unusual for proteins to be converted into carbohydrates and then to fat. So the type of food you consume is important. As far as timing is concerned, in many experiments, it has been shown that people who skip breakfast and/or lunch but consume a large dinner are more prone to gain weight. On the other hand, those who eat small quantities of food throughout the day, even if they're consuming the same number of calories overall, maintain or even lose weight.

# III

# Medically Significant Obesity

## BODY COMPOSITION AND OBESITY

As we have increased our understanding of obesity, we have learned that an individual's body weight is not an accurate measure of body fat. A person's percentage of body fat is a more precise measure of his or her weight problem. There are a number of ways to measure body fat, some of these are given here.

"Eyeball"—If you look in the mirror, your body looks fat and flabby rather than fit and toned. You probably have excess fat.

"Pinch an Inch" method—If you can grab an inch or more of the extra flesh around your middle, you have excess fat.

"Skin Fold Thickness" is measured with a pair of calipers. This measurement is more relevant for younger people. Measurements can be taken in the triceps area on the upper arm or under the shoulder blade. This measurement is used in the weight loss programs to document the progress of weight loss.

## HEIGHT AND WEIGHT TABLE

Over the years, tables have been developed by the Metropolitan Life Insurance Company on expected weight for a certain height. These tables have served as a gold standard for normal ranges. You can look up your height in the table to find the range of weight that would be considered normal for you. While the table does not measure the body fat content, it can give a rough idea in most of the people.

## BODY MASS INDEX

Body mass index (BMI) is a very important measurement. This correlates more closely with the body fat percentage. BMI is commonly used in classifying obesity. You can get two important pieces of information from BMI: whether you are overweight or obese; and whether this obesity is putting you at higher risk for health problems. This level of obesity that causes health problems is called medically significant obesity.

Once you know your BMI, the next thing to be determined is the grade of obesity. In the following table there are different grades of obesity—from one to six.

The table also gives you approximately how much excess fat is in the body.

This table can also be used when you are losing weight to determine your grade of obesity.

In determining if being overweight is making you

## Metropolitan Life Height & Weight Table for Adults

| Height[†] | 19–34 y | | Over 35 y | |
|---|---|---|---|---|
| | Average | Range | Average | Range |
| In pounds | | | | |
| 5'0" | 112 | 97–128 | 123 | 108–138 |
| 5'1" | 116 | 101–132 | 127 | 111–143 |
| 5'2" | 120 | 104–137 | 131 | 115–148 |
| 5'3" | 124 | 107–141 | 135 | 119–152 |
| 5'4" | 128 | 111–146 | 140 | 122–157 |
| 5'5" | 132 | 114–150 | 144 | 126–162 |
| 5'6" | 136 | 118–155 | 148 | 130–167 |
| 5'7" | 140 | 121–160 | 153 | 134–172 |
| 5'8" | 144 | 125–164 | 158 | 138–178 |
| 5'9" | 149 | 129–169 | 162 | 142–183 |
| 5'10" | 153 | 132–174 | 167 | 146–188 |
| 5'11" | 157 | 136–179 | 172 | 151–194 |
| 6'0" | 162 | 140–184 | 177 | 155–199 |
| 6'1" | 166 | 144–189 | 182 | 159–205 |
| 6'2" | 171 | 148–195 | 187 | 164–210 |
| 6'3" | 176 | 152–200 | 192 | 168–216 |
| 6'4" | 180 | 156–205 | 197 | 173–222 |
| 6'5" | 185 | 160–211 | 202 | 177–228 |
| 6'6" | 190 | 164–216 | 208 | 182–234 |
| In kilograms | | | | |
| 152 | 51 | 44–58 | 55 | 49–62 |
| 155 | 53 | 46–60 | 58 | 50–65 |
| 157 | 54 | 47–62 | 59 | 52–67 |
| 160 | 56 | 49–64 | 61 | 54–69 |
| 163 | 58 | 51–66 | 64 | 56–72 |
| 165 | 60 | 52–68 | 65 | 57–74 |
| 168 | 62 | 54–71 | 68 | 59–76 |
| 170 | 64 | 55–72 | 69 | 61–78 |
| 173 | 66 | 57–75 | 72 | 63–81 |
| 175 | 67 | 58–77 | 74 | 64–83 |
| 178 | 70 | 60–79 | 76 | 67–86 |
| 180 | 71 | 62–81 | 78 | 68–88 |
| 183 | 74 | 64–84 | 80 | 70–90 |
| 185 | 75 | 65–86 | 82 | 72–92 |
| 188 | 78 | 67–88 | 85 | 74–95 |
| 191 | 80 | 69–91 | 88 | 77–99 |
| 193 | 82 | 71–93 | 89 | 78–101 |
| 196 | 85 | 73–96 | 92 | 81–104 |
| 198 | 86 | 75–98 | 94 | 82–106 |
| BMI $(kg/m^2)$ | 22 | 19–25 | 24 | 21–27 |

*Without clothes. Derived from National Research Council, 1985
[†] Without shoes.

Reprinted with permission. *American Journal of Clinical Nutrition*, 1992.

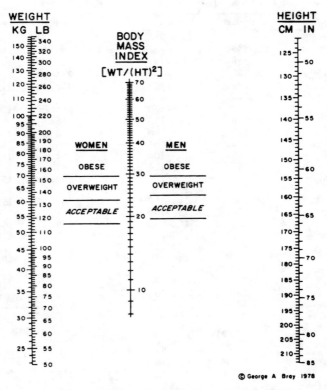

NOMOGRAM FOR BODY MASS INDEX

Nomogram for determining BMI. Lay a straight-line across between weight and height. The point where it crosses the BMI line is the BMI in metric units (kg/m²). (Copyright 1978 George A. Bray, MD; reproduced with permission.)

sick, your grade of BMI is an important measure but it has to be correlated with other existing obesity-related health problems. For example, a BMI of 25 is normal and by itself is very low risk, but if there are complicating health problems like high blood pressure, heart attack or diabetes mel-

## Medical Classification of Obesity Using Body Mass Index (BMI)[*†]

| Desirable Weight (%) | Definition | Grade of Obesity | Excess Fat (lb/kg) | BMI (kg/m²) |
|---|---|---|---|---|
| **Men** | | | | |
| 225 | Super morbid obesity | 6 | 175/80 | ≥50 |
| 200 | Morbid obesity | 5 | 145/66 | 45 |
| 180 | Super obesity | 4 | 110/50 | 40 |
| 160 | Medically significant obesity | 3 | 80/36 | 35 |
| 135 | Obesity | 2 | 50/23 | 30 |
| 110 | Overweight | 1 | 15/7 | 25 |
| 100 | Desirable weight | 0 | 0 | 22 |
| 70 | Medically significant starvation | −3 | −15/−7[‡] | 15 |
| **Women** | | | | |
| 245 | Super morbid obesity | 6 | 155/70 | ≥50 |
| 220 | Morbid obesity | 5 | 130/59 | 45 |
| 195 | Super obesity | 4 | 100/45 | 40 |
| 170 | Medically significant obesity | 3 | 75/34 | 35 |
| 145 | Obesity | 2 | 50/23 | 30 |
| 120 | Overweight | 1 | 25/11 | 25 |
| 100 | Desirable weight | 0 | 0 | 21 |
| 75 | Medically significant starvation | −3 | −20/−9[‡] | 15 |

[*]Medical Risk of obesity is further modified by concurrent illness(es), complicating organ dysfunction, body fat distribution, velocity of weight change and age. Relative risk varies from 2- to 15-fold.

[†]Excess fat (pounds), assuming 90% excess body weight is fat plus extracellular water.

Assuming 75% of weight loss in simple starvation is body fat.

desirable weight = % desirable body weight = 154 pounds for Reference Man; 120 pounds for Reference Woman (1980 Recommended Dietary Allowance Table)

Body mass index was developed by the Nutrition/Metabolism Laboratory, Cancer Research Institute, Boston, Massachusetts.

Adapted with permission from *American Journal of Cardiology Supplement.*

litus, the risk goes to a higher level. A BMI of 25–30 is normally low risk, but in the presence of complicating factors it becomes a moderate risk and so risk keeps increasing. After determining your BMI you look at the medical classification of obesity table and determine your grade of obe-

| | Body Mass Index |
|---|---|
| Age Group (yr) | 19–24 |
| 25–34 | 20–25 |
| 35–44 | 21–26 |
| 45–54 | 22–27 |
| 55–64 | 23–28 |
| 65+ | 24–29 |

The Classification and Evaluation of Obesity
Desirable Body Mass Index Range in Relation to Age

From Bray.[1] Reproduced by permission.
Body mass index can be determined from the nomogram in figure on page 14.

sity and how much excess fat you have. This will help you to know where you are right now and you can set up goals for yourself for weight loss. You can also look in the table for the desirable BMI.

## Waist To Hip Ratio:

The waist to hip measurements are important in risk measurement.

BMI gives a good overall assessment about the body fat. Even more important than the body fat content is how the fat is distributed in the body. In men the fat accumulates in a "pot belly" or "spare tire" pattern in the abdomen. This fat pattern is associated with high risk for cardiovascular disease, atherosclerosis and cancer. In women most of the fat accumulates in the hips which is considered "noble fat;" this fat does not increase the risk for cardiovascular disease but can cause degenerative arthritis in knees and ankles due to wear and tear of joints and due to sheer overweight.

Men with a waist to hip measurement over 0.9 are

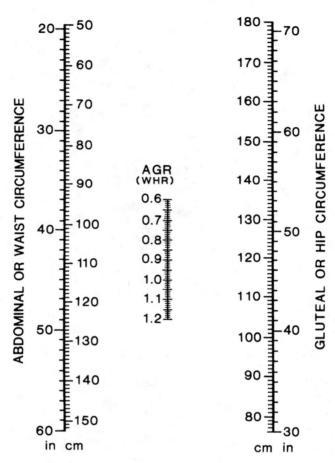

Nomogram for determining abdominal (waist) to gluteal (hips) ratio. Place a straight line between the column for waist circumference and the column for hip circumference and read the ratio from the point where this straight edge crosses the AGR or WHR line. The waist or abdominal circumference is the smallest circumference beneath the rib cage and above the umbilicus, and the hips or gluteal circumference is taken as the largest circumference at the posterior extension of the buttocks. (© George A. Bray, 1987. Reproduced with permission.)

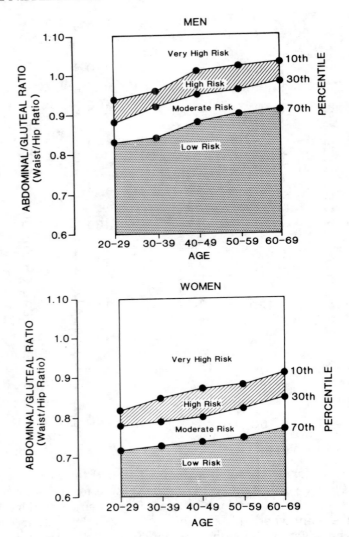

Percentiles for fat distribution. The percentiles for the ratio of abdominal circumference to gluteal circumference (ratio of waist to hips) are depicted for men (A) and women (B) by age groups. The relative risk associated with these percentiles is indicated, based on the available information. (Plotted from tabular data in the Canadian Standardized Test of Fitness, 3rd ed., 1986. © George A. Bray, 1987). Printed with permission.

more prone to heart disease, high blood pressure, stroke, diabetes mellitus and some forms of cancer. Women with waist to hip ratios over 0.8 are at risk for these same diseases. This ratio is considered an independent and serious predictor for these illnesses. A recent study examined more than 30,000 healthy women aged 50 to 69. Over the course of one year there were three times more heart attacks and deaths in women with waist to hip ratios greater than 0.86 as compared to women with smaller ratios of 0.85

# HEALTH RISKS OF OBESITY

Obesity is a very serious health concern that markedly decreases the quality of life for many people. Obesity is one of the major factors of premature death in the United States and is generally believed to contribute to 300,000 deaths each year. Because of the increased risk for diabetes, heart disease and cancer, individuals who are 50% over their ideal weight have twice the risk of premature death.[15] The mortality rate keeps on going higher as the weight class climbs. In patients with extreme obesity the mortality is as high as 1200% when compared to normal-weight persons. Recent research indicates that the distribution of fat is a more important predictor of mortality than the body mass index or total body weight.[16] These are some of the serious health risks associated with obesity:

*Coronary Artery Disease:* Coronary artery disease (CAD) is the leading cause of death and sickness among Americans. More Americans die from cardiovascular disease than all other diseases combined. More than 500,000 Americans die from CAD and its consequences each year. Almost 70% of the adult population is affected to some extent. The financial cost—direct (care of patients) and indirect

19

(lost productivity)—is greater than $117.4 billion a year, according to the American Heart Association. A number of studies—Framingham Heart Study, American Cancer Society, Veterans, Nurses' Health Study, Harvard Alumni— have documented the relationship between obesity and increased risk of cardiovascular disease. Deaths due to CAD are 50% higher among overweight individuals than among those of normal weight. The figure rises to 90% in morbidly obese individuals.[17] The causes of cardiovascular disease are well understood. High blood pressure, smoking, diabetes mellitus, elevated serum cholesterol, family history and obesity are well known independent risk factors. Obesity is an underlying factor in high blood pressure, diabetes mellitus and elevated serum cholesterol so controlling obesity will help directly by reducing the load on the heart and indirectly by reducing the other risk factors.

*Hypertension:* High blood pressure has a strong relationship to being overweight. Blood pressure goes up as a person gains weight and decreases as soon as he or she loses weight. The incidence of hypertension in adults 20 to 75 years old is three times higher in overweight people as compared to normal-weight persons. Broken down by smaller age groups, the relative risk of high blood pressure is almost six times greater in 20 to 45 year olds who are overweight. The risk is double for those 45 to 75 years old.[18] Losing weight will lower blood pressure and decrease the need for medications to control hypertension.

*Diabetes Mellitus:* Insulin is the messenger that transports blood sugar into cells. Diabetes mellitus develops either due to the body's inability to produce sufficient insulin or its inability to function properly when insulin is produced. A high food intake leads to higher levels of insulin. Obesity leads to decreased sensitivity of the receptors on the cells to insulin. The insulin becomes less able to transport sugar to cells. Overweight adults, aged 20 to 75, have three times the risk of developing type II diabetes as compared to their normal-weight peers. The risk is higher for young overweight people also. In the 20- to 45-year age group, the risk of type II diabetes among overweight persons is four times that of normal-weight persons.[18] To control type II diabetes, individuals must reduce their weight and maintain a proper calorie intake, exercise and take insulin or oral hypoglycemic agents if they have been prescribed.

*Cholesterol*: Obesity is related to high serum cholesterol. The relative risk of high blood cholesterol for overweight Americans aged 25 to 70 is 1.5 times that of persons who are not overweight. The risk is even higher in younger age groups. For example, overweight Americans aged 25 to 45 are twice as likely to have high cholesterol levels.[18] Many studies have shown a direct relationship between elevated blood cholesterol and an increased risk of coronary heart disease. There is overwhelming evidence that lowering cholesterol with diet and medications will reduce that risk.[19] Lowering your cholesterol will decrease your risk of developing angina or a heart attack and reverse atherosclerosis. Nibbler's Diet™ is an excellent way to reduce cholesterol with or without drug therapy as determined by your physician.

*Stroke*: Approximately 500,000 Americans suffer a stroke annually. The incidence continues to rise each year. This number was only 400,000 in 1983. Improved treatment and prevention have helped decrease morbidity by more than 50% over the past 15 years, but 150,000 Americans still die from strokes each year and an even greater number suffer severe disability. The risk factors for stroke are

Common Causes of Death: The Diet Connection

| Cause of death | No. of deaths (1,000) | Death rate per 100,000 |
|---|---|---|
| **Hypertensive and ischemic heart disease** | **521.3** | **210.0** |
| **Malignancies** | **496.2** | **199.9** |
| **Cerebrovascular diseases** | **145.6** | **58.6** |
| Accidents (motor vehicle and others) and adverse effects | 95.0 | 38.3 |
| Chronic obstructive pulmonary diseases and allied conditions | 84.3 | 34.0 |
| Pneumonia and influenza | 76.6 | 30.8 |
| **Diabetes mellitus** | **46.8** | **18.9** |
| Suicide | 30.2 | 12.2 |
| **Chronic liver disease and cirrhosis** | **26.7** | **10.8** |
| **Atherosclerosis** | **19.4** | **7.8** |

Note: The causes of death in which diet is a factor are in boldface. These statistics are for 1989.

Source: *Statistical Abstract of the United States: 1992*, ed 112. Bureau of the Census, 1992.

diabetes mellitus, high blood pressure, and elevated cholesterol levels. Obesity indirectly causes strokes. Controlling weight will control all the risk factors and reduce the risk of stroke.[20]

*Pregnancy complications:* Obesity has significant effects on the metabolism of hormones. This can decrease ovulation and decrease the chance of becoming pregnant. Even after becoming pregnant there are numerous complications such as high blood pressure, toxemia and pre-toxemia, gestational diabetes mellitus, abnormal presentation of the fetus and abnormally large amount of bleeding after delivery. These contribute to a higher rate of cesarean section births among overweight women.[21] Preliminary research suggests that obesity is also linked to birth defects such as spina bifida.[22]

*Gallbladder disease:* Medical students are taught four risk factors for gallbladder disease—female, fat, forty, fetus. A woman over 40 who is overweight and has had children is at higher risk of developing gallbladder disease. This is mainly due to the higher concentration of cholesterol in bile in obese people. This also increases the risk for gallbladder cancer.

*Cancer:* Numerous studies have shown an increased incidence of cancer in obese subjects. Among males the cancers related to obesity are colon, rectal and prostate. In obese women, there are higher rates of breast, uterine, ovarian and gallbladder cancer. Women with upper body fat patterns (apple shape) are six times more likely to develop breast cancer compared to women who are pear shaped.[16] The risk for cancer can be reduced through proper diet and exercise.

*Arthritis*: Arthritis is inflammation of joints and causes stiffness and pain. There are a number of arthritic conditions associated with overweight—degenerative, gouty and carpal tunnel syndrome.

> *Degenerative arthritis* is due to increased stress caused by excess weight on weight-bearing joints like the knees, lower part of the spine, hips and ankles. Wear and tear on these joints leads to pain, stiffness

and decreased mobility and poor quality of life. Recent research has shown that degenerative arthritis associated with obesity not only affects the weight-bearing joints but also the small joints of the hands. University of Michigan researchers at a small town in Michigan found that respondents who were 20% or more overweight were three times more likely to have degenerative arthritis of the hands.

*Gouty arthritis* can also be related to being overweight. A recent Johns Hopkins study showed that obesity (during adulthood) and hypertension are potentially modifiable risk factors for developing gouty arthritis. Gout is brought on by an increased load of uric acid (a break-down product of the body). Normally the kidneys can filter this acid into the urine without difficulty, but when there is an excessive load, the uric acid backs up into the blood and crystallizes in a joint.[25]

*Carpal tunnel syndrome* is another arthritic condition associated with being overweight. A study in Oregon in 1992 showed that obesity was the most serious risk factor for carpal tunnel syndrome which affects the nerves at the wrist.

*Immune system:* Obesity is known to weaken the immune system making persons more vulnerable to infection. This may also be a contributing factor to the development of cancer. A recent Japanese study found that losing weight can boost the immune system as measured by the T-lymphocytes in the blood—the body's defenders against infections.

There is a wide body of research that shows moderate weight loss (10–15% of body weight) decreases health hazards and medical problems in 90% of obese patients. This results in improvement in heart function, lowers blood pressure, lowers blood sugar in diabetes mellitus, decreases sleep disturbances and improves cholesterol, lowers the need for multiple medications and decreases the length of hospital stays and the number of postoperative complications. For women, the risk for cardiovascular disease decreases with moderate weight loss even if they remain obese.[27]

Very important research in this area called the Framingham Study showed that a 10% reduction in body weight may result in a 20% reduction in the risk of developing coronary artery disease.[28]

## OBESITY AND MENTAL HEALTH

Obesity can lead to poor self-esteem, increased anxiety and depression. It can lead to social isolation. Individuals can be caught in a vicious cycle in which they eat to relieve anxiety, gain more weight, feel further social rejection and experience an even greater decrease in self-esteem.

A life-time of negative feedback can contribute to psychological problems. Overweight children are often subject to cruel taunts. This intense prejudice can set up individuals for a lifetime of feelings of low self-worth.

As obese children become overweight adults, they face discrimination. Excess weight can affect success at work, ability to obtain life and health insurance, college placement and employment opportunities. In one study, 16% of employers said they would not hire obese women under any circumstances; another 50% said they would hire them only under special circumstances. A study of corporate executives showed that each pound of excess fat cost an executive $1,000 a year in salary.[29] The armed forces, police and fire departments and airlines will not hire obese people and will discharge those who do not conform to guidelines.

The intense scrutiny obese people receive can create feelings of shame. These negative feelings can lead to binge eating, more obesity and more depression, anxiety and obsessive behavior.

# IV

# NIBBLER'S DIET™: SUCCESS STORIES

## THE NIBBLER'S DIET™ PLAN

### Winners and Losers in the Weight-Loss Game

Many fortunes have been made on the road to the perfect weight-loss plan. Some of the programs are based on sound principles; others can do more harm than good. You don't want to do harm as you seek a slimmer body. Many years ago, some patients went on a formula diet and some of our colleagues distributed this diet to their patients. This diet provided only 300 calories a day with very poor-quality protein. This is a starvation diet. Such a low calorie intake causes the muscles to break down as they starve for the proteins they need. Some of these patients experienced very slow heart beats as their hearts, which are muscles also, lost function. A number of patients around the country died due to irregular heart beats and eventually the diet fell out of favor.

Weight gain or obesity is the result of many years of poor habits. To make the widespread changes needed to lose a substantial amount of weight, one needs to rethink the entire life-style. The quick fixes just won't work.

Put your weight-loss efforts into activities that will make a difference. Pick solutions that are sensible and that will really work. It may be discouraging to realize there aren't any fast and magical solutions. But by starting today on a realistic and sensible plan, you are making sure that a week from now, a month from now, a year from now and forever you will feel better, look better and be more fit.

To be successful in meeting your fitness goals, you must utilize the principles of the Nibbler's Diet™ to overcome these obstacles:

- A metabolic rate that tends to store calories and fat
- High proportion of body fat
- Low proportion of lean body mass
- Habits and self-opinion detrimental to your own well being

The Nibbler's Diet™ plan will help you by:

- Lowering body fat and cholesterol
- Increasing your lean body mass
- Increasing your metabolic rate so you burn more calories and store fewer calories in the form of fat
- Giving you a greater feeling of zest making exercise and activity goals easier to achieve
- Providing a way for you to succeed and breaking the destructive cycle of failed dieting

Patients on the Nibbler's Diet™ eating frequent, small meals all day have decreased their body weight, increased their muscle mass and lowered their body fat content and lowered cholesterol.

## WHEN WEIGHT LOSS IS MANDATORY

1. Medically significant obesity is when you weigh 20% in excess of desirable weight. This is equal to a body mass index of 25.8 for women and 26.9 for men.

2. Family history or risk factors for Type II Diabetes Mellitus.

3. High blood pressure.

4. High triglyceride level or high cholesterol.

5. Angina or coronary artery disease.

6. Gout.

7. Inability to function properly due to heart disease, emphysema, or osteoarthritis in weight bearing joints like spine, hips, knees, and ankles.

8. History of childhood obesity.

9. Sleep apnea.[32]

## HOW MUCH WEIGHT YOU NEED TO LOSE

There are number of ways to determine how much weight you need to lose:

1. Roughly you can see from weight and weight tables.

*"It hurts when I huff and puff."*

Courtesy Joyce Buttons. Printed with permission.

2. BMI table to assess body mass index.

3. Use the obesity classification table to see how many pounds you need to lose.

After you have determined how much you need to lose, you need to set a plan to lose the weight in steps. For example, if you need to lose 50 lbs then plan to lose 25 lbs in 2–3 months. After weight has stabilized, then go on a higher calorie maintenance plan for 6 months. Then after 6 months, start lower calorie menu and lose the remaining 25 lbs in subsequent 3 months.

# EXERCISE AND WEIGHT LOSS

Obesity develops as a result of overeating but recent research has made it clear that a sedentary lifestyle is also a
major contributor. People generally lose about 1% lean
body mass every year after the age of 40 and gain a pound
of fat every year. As you get older, it becomes even more
important to stay active. Exercise has many positive effects
on the body. It produces endorphins, a natural drug, that
creates a feeling of euphoria. This feeling is often called a
"jogger's high." Exercise improves the muscles, increasing
lean mass and decreasing fat. The Approximate Energy Expenditures of Recreational Sports table lists a number of
activities with their calorie expenditures.[30]

A favorite activity of many people is exercise walking. It is gentler to the muscles, cartilages and joints than
other forms of exercise. All you need is a pair of sneakers
and a place to walk.

It's recommended that you start slowly, walking 10 or
15 minutes a day. Gradually increase the length and vigor
of your exercise sessions. You should gradually work up to
1 hour of exercise three times a week. If you want to do
strenuous exercise aerobically, do so for 30-40 minutes at
least three to four times a week. Some of the tips that our
patients have found to be helpful include:

- Pair up with an exercise partner who will help to
  keep you motivated.

- Find forms of exercise that you enjoy.

- Start slowly and build up your activity level. Many
  people exhaust themselves in the beginning because
  they work too hard and then give up entirely rather
  than finding a reasonable activity level.

- Vary your activities to keep them interesting and

TABLE 1. Approximate Energy Expenditures of Recreational Sports

| Activity | Kcal per hour* | Activity | Kcal per hour* |
|---|---|---|---|
| Baseball/softball | | Skiing | |
| All except pitcher | 280 | Downhill, light | 500 |
| Pitcher | 450 | Downhill, vigorous | 600 |
| | | Cross country, 2.5 mph | 360 |
| Basketball | 360–660 | Cross country, 4 mph | 600 |
| | | Cross country, 5 mph | 700 |
| Bicycling | | Cross country, 8 mph | 1,020 |
| 5 mph | 240 | | |
| 8 mph | 300 | Swimming | |
| 10 mph | 420 | Leisurely | 360–500 |
| 11 mph | 480 | Crawl, 25–50 yard per | |
| 12 mph | 600 | minute | 360–750 |
| 13 mph | 660 | Backstroke, 25–50 yard | |
| | | per minute | 360–750 |
| Calisthenics | | Breaststroke, 25–50 yard | |
| Light | 360 | per minute | 260–750 |
| Heavy | 600 | Butterfly, 50 yard per | |
| | | minute | 840 |
| Golfing | | Sidestroke, 40 yard | |
| Powercart | 240 | per minute | 660 |
| Pulling bag cart | 300 | | |
| Carrying clubs | 360 | Tennis | |
| | | Doubles | 360 |
| Handball | | Singles | 480 |
| Social | 600 | | |
| Competitive | 660 | Volleyball | |
| | | Noncompetitive | 300 |
| Rowing machine | 840 | Competitive | 480 |
| | | | |
| Running | | Walking | |
| 5 mph (jogging) | 600 | Level road, 1–2 mph | |
| 6 mph (jogging) | 750 | (strolling) | 120–150 |
| 7 mph (moderate) | 870 | Level road, 3 mph | |
| 8 mph (moderate) | 1,020 | (leisurely) | 300 |
| 9 mph (fast) | 1,130 | Level road, 3.5 mph | |
| 10 mph (very fast) | 1,285 | (brisk) | 360 |
| Upstairs, uphill | 1,100 | Level road, 4 mph (fast) | 420 |
| | | Level road, 5 mph | |
| Skating (ice, roller) | | (very fast) | 480 |
| Leisurely | 420 | Downstairs | 425 |
| Rapidly | 700 | Upstairs | 600–1080 |
| | | Uphill, 3.5 mph | 480–900 |
| | | Downhill, 2.5 mph | 240 |

*Caloric consumption is based on a person weighing 70 kg (150 lb). There is a 10 percent increase in caloric consumption for each 7 kg (15 lb) over this weight and a 10 percent decrease for each 7 kg under 70 kg.

Data from Bannister and Brown, Howley and Glover, and Passmore and Durnin. Reprinted with permission from the June, 1993 issue of *American Family Physician*, published by the American Academy of Family Physicians.

*"Join a gym! You're not getting enough exercise chasing rallies in the stock market.*

Courtesy Aaron Bacall. Printed with permission.

fresh. Try different workout videos, walk different routes, swim, roller skate, join an exercise class.

- Make exercise a priority and set aside time during the week just as you would for a business or social appointment.

- Exercise at least three times each week.

- Be consistent. To achieve consistency, find a form of exercise that you really enjoy and can stick with.

- The best approach to exercise is to start slowly. As

you become more fit, add strength training and weights or resistance machines.

## HOW EXERCISE HELPS

The body burns calories day and night—while we're active and at rest. Even when we're least active, we use calories to maintain our basic body functions. These calories are used by the components that make up our lean body mass—organs, muscles and bones. The greater the proportion of muscle we have, the more calories we burn going about even our normal daily activities. In contrast, fat is very efficient and stores calories.

Exercise has a wonderful effect on burning calories. People who exercise moderately for an hour burn 8% more calories during the day than people who do not exercise. High endurance athletes can burn up to 14% more calories than sedentary people.

## THE NIBBLER'S DIET™

The Nibbler's Diet™ mobilizes the fat you have stored to meet your energy needs. As you use up your stores of fat, you lose weight and begin to build your lean muscle mass.

It takes 3,500 calories to lose or gain one pound of fat. On the Nibbler's Diet™ you can expect to lose about three and a half pounds of weight a week as you decrease your calorie intake and increase your exercise level.

There are enough calories in the diet to maintain a high metabolic rate. Your body will not move into "starvation" mode where it tries to compensate for a low calorie intake by holding onto its fat reserves. As you stay with

*"It's 10 P.M.. Do you know how many pounds you have to lose?"*

Courtesy Aaron Bacall. Printed with permission.

the diet, your metabolism will adjust to the program and will sustain your weight loss.

The Nibbler's Diet™ is based on small quantities of food eaten throughout the day. Over time, this will help to decrease your appetite. This also stimulates the metabolism to burn the food as fast as possible.

Our experience with our patients has been that they feel there is too much food to eat so they are more than satisfied with the quantity of food. It is also easy to follow because it is based on readily available food. It is inexpensive without any requirements for special foods or supplements. It is easy to follow.

Experiments in laboratory animals have shown that timing of food intake has a significant effect on metabolism. Mice fed regular meals were compared to mice allowed to nibble the same amount of food all day. The mice fed regular meals showed an increased capacity to store energy, implying a gain in body fat.[30]

Similar studies of food intake on people have shown that skin fold thickness is related to the frequency of food intake. Excessive weight gain increased skin fold thickness in groups consuming three or less meals a day as compared to a group of people who consumed five or more meals a day. Those consuming four meals a day were in the middle.

In another study, a prominent obesity researcher found that gorging and nibbling have different effects on lipogenesis (fat storage). He found that the frequency of food intake was inversely related to obesity.[31]

Our experience in the private practice has been very similar. Our patients who followed the Nibbler's Diet™ consistently lost weight due to a low-fat diet consumed in eight small meals each day.

## HOW TO PSYCHE YOURSELF FOR SUCCESS

Most of us, along with unhealthy eating habits, have developed unhealthy messages to ourselves. We have ambitions, goals and dreams of becoming thin, of sticking to an exercise plan, of dealing with the issues that prevent us from living full lives. Unfortunately, the messages we tell ourselves are often more along the line:

- "I'm not capable."

- "I've tried before and failed."

- "There's too many other things going on for me to deal with this now."

These negative messages become self-fulfilling prophecies and handy excuses. You can take your goals and put them into action. Do you recall the last time you wanted something very badly—a new car? a house? a new outfit? To attain it you put together a plan. You evaluated. You recognized that there were trade-offs. Maybe you had to give up something in order to save for the important thing you really wanted.

You can identify ways you have been successful in your life. If you can achieve in one area, you can also achieve your weight-loss and fitness goals.

Approach your diet with a determined but relaxed attitude. Don't let minor setbacks deter you. You don't have to be perfect—only committed and centered on your ultimate goal. When you start to give yourself negative messages, consider the things you have done well. If you allow yourself to become stressed, you will be less likely to stick to your plan.

Identify hobbies, activities and social pursuits that will help keep you occupied and happy and will reinforce the positive things you know about yourself. Nurture relationships that are loving and caring.

Recognize that your perception of how you look is not a measure of your worth.

## WHAT OTHERS SAY ABOUT
## THE NIBBLER'S DIET™

Many individuals have been successful using the Nibbler's Diet™ to reach their health goals. These are the experiences of some of our patients:

"On your diet I lost 50 pounds in four months and reduced my cholesterol level substantially. The diet is

so well balanced that it does not leave me hungry.
Plus I like the variety of foods I can eat. Thank you.

James M. Bresko

"I am writing to thank you for letting me be a part of
your Nibbler's Diet™. I had added quite a few pounds
in the last two years and have had a difficult time losing them. I started the Nibbler's Diet™ with my husband, Raymond, after he had his heart attack. We
were both having trouble sticking to the other diet he
was on so we decided to give yours a try. We started
not quite believing we would feel satisfied. To our
surprise, we not only lost weight but felt full all the
time. We both enjoy our food. And we are both enjoy-
ing the diet. We are amazed that we can graze all day
long and still lose weight."

Linda Garrison

"I have tried to lose weight through every group plan
and special diet imaginable. I have found that yours is
the one that has worked best for me. What I particularly like is the variety and eight times a day I can
have something to eat. I'm 70 years old and am taking
care of my house and my husband who is handi-
capped plus I exercise two days a week. I really feel
so much better and am able to stay active since I've
been eating this way."

Jane James

## STARTING THE NIBBLERS' DIET™
## AND EXERCISE PLAN

Day-by-day menus are presented here. There are menus for
1000-, 1200-, 1500- and 1800-calorie diets.

You should check with your doctor before beginning a diet and exercise program. Your doctor can help you determine a safe level of physical activity and the proper calorie level. A general guide is that the average woman can start out with the 1000 calorie plan; after she has reached her goal then she can move on to 1200 calories or higher to maintain her weight. The average man may start out with the 1200 calorie or 1500 calorie plan; after the goal weight is achieved he can move onto the higher caloric level.

Remember, diet and exercise must occur simultaneously for proper weight loss results and fitness.

Vary your diet to ensure you get a good mix of nutrients. Variety will also help you keep interested in the diet and will make it easier for you to eat wisely. You can mix the menus; if one day's selections don't appeal to you, you have the option of switching to another menu.

Measuring your food is essential. The size of "servings" has grown over the years and we have become accustomed to bountiful restaurant meals, like "all you can eat for certain number of dollars," heaping plates and seconds and thirds. Retrain your eye to recognize a serving by carefully measuring your food according to the menu suggestions. The proportions in the Nibbler's Diet™ are based on recommendations from the Food Guide Pyramid.

All the plans are set up for eating every 2 hours of so.

## Making Smart Choices at the Grocery Store

When shopping for your food, be sure to:

Buy the cuts of meat specified on the menu.
Canned fruit should be packed in its own juice or water.
Fruit juice should be 100% natural. You do not want juice that contains corn syrup, high fructose corn

syrup, sugar, glucose-fructose syrup or sucrose syrup listed as ingredients. 100% fruit juice from concentrate is a good choice.

Fresh or frozen vegetables are recommended. If you are buying canned vegetables, select those labeled "low sodium" or "no salt added." If a product has more than 300 mg of sodium per serving, it is not a low-sodium item.

Tuna should be packed in water, not oil. The difference is fat calories.

## Making Smart Choices in the Kitchen

The menus are written without the addition of fat in cooking. Use non-stick pans and use non-stick cooking spray instead of cooking in margarine, butter or oil. Adding water to the skillet can also help keep meat from sticking. Remove the skin from turkey and chicken before cooking.

Salt and spices that contain salt (garlic salt, celery salt, etc.) are not recommended. Use salt substitutes and experiment with herbs and spices. You can shake your salt habit. Use your imagination and you can come up with some great flavors. Here are some recommendations:

*Fruits*
Allspice
Cinnamon
Nutmeg
Ginger
Mint flakes
Cloves

*Poultry*
Rosemary
Thyme

Marjoram
Onion powder
Garlic powder
Cumin
Bay leaf
Tarragon

*Pork*
Garlic powder
Onion powder
Sage

Thyme
Red pepper
Caraway
Oregano
Bay leaf
Tarragon

*Beef*
Dry mustard
Garlic powder
Onion powder
Instant minced onion
Black pepper
Red pepper

Oregano
Dill

*Vegetables*
Basil
Rosemary
Red pepper
Cinnamon
Nutmeg
Garlic pepper
Onion powder
Dill
Celery seed
Curry powder

## About Beverages

Although we have not specified beverages in the daily menus, we recommend you drink at least eight 8-ounce glasses of water a day. It is best to drink a glass of water before each meal. For those who have difficulty drinking water, here are some suggestions to ensure an adequate fluid intake:

Add lemon or lime to your water to give it a bit of taste.

Substitute decaffeinated coffee or tea (hot or cold) without sugar or cream.

Try diet soft drinks or sugar-free drink mixes. (A word of caution: sometimes when individuals consume drinks with artificial sweeteners, because of the intensity of the sweetness, they actually trigger a craving for sweet foods.) Although we do allow these diet beverages, we recommend you use them in moderation.

There are several benefits to drinking ample amounts of water each day. By drinking a glass of water before each meal you will achieve a feeling of fullness, enabling you to eat less food but still feel satisfied. Liquids also help your kidneys function properly and remove waste. If you tend to retain water, consuming an adequate amount of water will help "flush" your system, removing excess sodium which contributes to fluid retention.

## Unlimited Foods

Here are some foods which you can use as you desire.

### Beverages
Decaffeinated tea and coffee
Low-fat/low-sodium broth
Low-sodium bouillon

### Vegetables
Spinach
Lettuce

### Sugar Substitutes
Sugar-free hard candy
Sugar-free gum
Sugar-free gelatin
Sugar substitutes (Sweet-n-Low, Equal, Sugar-Twin)

### Condiments
Mustard
Ketchup (limit 2 to 3 tbsp. per day)
Horseradish
Low-sodium worcestershire sauce (limit to 1 tbsp. per day)
Picante sauce (limit to 3 tbsp. per day)
Non stick cooking spray

# V

# 1000 CALORIES
## SHOPPING LIST AND MENUS

## WEEK 1

### Meats
Chicken breast
Tuna packed in water
Ground sirloin
Turkey breast
Ham
Flank steak
Egg substitute
Fish

### Fruits
Cantaloupe
Pineapple or canned
   pineapple chunks
   packed in water or
   own juice
Pears
Grapes
Grapefruit
Peaches or canned
peaches packed in
   water or own juice
Fruit cocktail packed
   in water or own
   juice
Oranges

### Breads/starches
Pancake mix (complete
   pancake mix or
   frozen pancakes
   with less than 2
   grams of fat)
Saltine crackers
Potatoes
Noodles
Bran Flakes cereal
Bagel
Hamburger bun
Whole wheat bread

Pretzels
Graham crackers
Pita bread (6″ across)
White rice
Popcorn
Vanilla wafers
Frozen soft pretzel

## Vegetables

Canned tomatoes
Green onion
Cucumber
Green pepper
Broccoli
Spinach
Tomato juice
Green beans
Carrots
Lettuce
Tomato
Celery

Radishes
Cauliflower
Corn
Peas

## Dairy products

Skim milk
Low-fat cottage cheese
Fat-free cheese
Non-fat frozen yogurt

## Miscellaneous/ condiments

Diet jelly
Diet syrup
Pickles
Miracle Whip (fat free)
    or fat-free margarine
Molly McButter
Fat-free cream cheese

## WEEK 1: SUNDAY

### 1000 Calories

1    2 pancakes (4″ across)
1 tbsp. light syrup
1 cup skim milk

2    1/3 cup cantaloupe

3    1 cup vegetable soup (see recipe)
6 saltine crackers

4    1/2 cup cottage cheese (low fat)

5    1 baked potato
1/2 cup steamed broccoli
1/2 cup skim milk

6    2 oz. chicken breast
1 cup noodles
1/2 cup spinach
1/2 cup skim milk

7    1/2 cup tomato juice

8    1/2 cup frozen non-fat yogurt
1/3 cup pineapple

# WEEK 1: MONDAY

## 1000 Calories

1    1/2 cup Bran Flakes
      1/2 cup skim milk

2    1/2 cup orange juice

3    1/2 cup tuna
      1 tsp. Miracle Whip (fat free)
      1 bagel

4    1/2 cup tomato juice

5    1 pear

6    2 oz. lean ground sirloin
      1 hamburger bun
      1 cup green beans
      1/2 cup skim milk

7    8 oz. fat-free yogurt

8    15 grapes

# WEEK 1: TUESDAY

## 1000 Calories

1.   2 slices whole wheat toast
1 tsp. diet jelly
1 cup skim milk

2.   1/2 medium grapefruit

3.   1 oz. turkey breast
1 slice whole wheat bread
1 tsp. Miracle Whip (fat free)
1 cup carrot sticks

4.   1 peach or 1/2 canned peaches in water or own juice

5.   3/4 oz. pretzels

6.   3 oz. boiled ham
1 small baked potato (sprinkle with Molly McButter)
1 cup skim milk

7.   Salad:
1 cup lettuce
1/2 tomato
1/2 cucumber
1 tbsp. lemon juice

8.   3 graham crackers (2.5" squares)

# WEEK 1: WEDNESDAY

## 1000 Calories

1. 1/2 cup Bran Flakes
   1 cup skim milk

2. 1/2 cup orange juice

3. 1/4 cup tuna
   1 pita bread (6" across)
   1 tsp. Miracle Whip (fat free)
   1 medium tomato diced
   1/2 cup shredded lettuce (put inside pita)

4. 3 graham crackers (2.5" square)
   1 cup skim milk

5. 1 cup celery sticks

6. 3 oz. chicken breast
   1/3 cup (cooked) rice
   1/2 cup broccoli

7. 15 grapes

8. 3 cups (air popped) popcorn
   or microwave popcorn with less than 2
   grams of fat per 3 cups

# WEEK 1:  THURSDAY

## 1000 Calories

1   2 slices whole wheat toast
    1/2 cup skim milk
    2 tsp. diet jelly

2   1/2 grapefruit

3   2 oz. turkey breast
    1 slice whole wheat bread
    1 cup carrot sticks
    1 medium cucumber

4   1/2 cup non-fat yogurt

5   1/2 bagel
    1 tsp. fat-free cream cheese

6   2 oz. fat-free cheese
    2 slices whole wheat bread
    1 pickle
    1 cup skim milk

7   Salad: 1/2 cup lettuce
        1/2 cup spinach
        1/4 cup radish
        1/4 cup carrots
        1/4 cup broccoli
        1 tbsp. lemon juice

8   1/2 cup fruit cocktail in own juice or water

# WEEK 1: FRIDAY

## 1000 Calories

1   1/2 cup Bran Flakes
    1/2 cup skim milk

2   1/3 cantaloupe

3   2 oz. boiled ham
    2 slices whole wheat bread
    1/2 cup tomato juice

4   6 saltine crackers

5   1/2 cup raw cauliflower
    1/2 cup raw broccoli
    1 tbsp. fat-free dressing

6   2 oz. lean flank steak
    1/2 cup corn
    1/2 cup green beans
    1 cup skim milk

7   1 peach or 1/2 cup canned peaches in
       water or own juice

8   6 vanilla wafers
    1/2 cup skim milk

# WEEK 1: SATURDAY

## 1000 Calories

1    1/2 cup egg substitute
2 slices whole wheat toast

2    1 pear

3    8 oz. fat-free yogurt

4    Salad:
      1 cup lettuce
      1/2 cup spinach
      1/4 cup broccoli
      2 tbsp. parmesan cheese
1 tbsp. fat-free dressing

5    1 orange

6    2 oz. fish
2/3 cup (cooked) rice
1/2 cup peas
1 cup skim milk

7    1 cup carrot sticks

8    1 soft frozen pretzel
Diet pop

## WEEK 2

### Meats

- Ham
- Turkey breast
- Tuna packed in water
- Ground sirloin
- Low-fat turkey lunch meat
- Skinless chicken breast
- Fish
- Pork tenderloin
- Egg substitute
- Lean beef sirloin

### Fruits

- Orange juice
- Strawberries (if out of season substitute choice of canned fruit in water or own juice or frozen strawberries)
- Cantaloupe
- Apple
- Plums (if out of season substitute choice of canned fruit in water or own juice)
- Grapefruit
- Grapes
- Orange
- Prunes or raisins
- Fruit cocktail packed in water or own juice
- Pineapple chunks packed in water or own juice
- Blueberries (fresh or frozen)

### Breads/starches

- Bagels
- Whole wheat bread
- Popcorn
- Bran Flakes
- Pita Bread (6" across)
- Saltine crackers
- Hamburger bun
- Potato
- Vanilla wafers
- Graham crackers
- Noodles
- Rice (white)
- Pancake mix (complete pancake mix or frozen pancakes with less than 2 grams of fat)

### Vegetables

- Lettuce
- Spinach
- Green peppers
- Alfalfa sprouts
- Radishes
- Peas
- Corn
- Carrots

Celery
Cauliflower
Cucumber
Canned tomatoes
Green onion
Broccoli
Mushrooms
Asparagus
Green beans

## Dairy products

Skim milk
Non-fat yogurt
Fat-free cheese

Non-fat frozen yogurt
Low-fat cottage cheese

## Miscellaneous/ condiments

Lemon juice
Pickles
Miracle Whip (fat free) or mayonnaise
Fat-free salad dressing
Sugar-free pudding
Sugar-free gelatin

# WEEK 2: SUNDAY

## 1000 Calories

1    1 bagel
1 tsp. diet jelly
1/2 cup orange juice
1/2 cup skim milk

2    1/2 grapefruit

3    2 oz. boiled ham
1 slice whole wheat bread
1 cup celery sticks

4    1/4 cup whole strawberries or 1/2 cup choice of canned fruit in own juice or water

5    2 oz. turkey breast
2/3 cup (cooked) rice
1 cup skim milk

6    Salad:
     1 cup lettuce
     1/3 cup radish
     1/2 cup cauliflower
     1/3 cup green onion
     1/2 cup cucumber
1 tbsp fat-free dressing

7    4 oz. non-fat yogurt

8    3 cups (air popped) popcorn or microwave popcorn with less than 2 grams of fat per 3 cups

# WEEK 2: MONDAY

## 1000 Calories

1   1/2 cup Bran Flakes
    1/2 cup skim milk

2   1/3 cantaloupe

3   1 cup carrot sticks

4   1/4 cup tuna
    1/2 pita bread 6" across
    1 tbsp. Miracle Whip (fat free)
    1 pickle

5   1 cup vegetable soup (see recipe)
    6 saltine crackers

6   3 oz. lean ground sirloin hamburger
    1/2 hamburger bun
    1 serving steak fries (one medium potato,
       see recipe)
    1 cup skim milk

7   1 apple

8   6 vanilla wafers
    1/2 cup skim milk

# WEEK 2: TUESDAY

## 1000 Calories

1   1 slice whole wheat toast
    1 cup skim milk

2   1/2 cup orange juice

3   1 oz. turkey
    1 slice whole wheat bread

4   1 cup raw broccoli
    1 tbsp. fat-free dressing

5   3 graham crackers (2.5" square)

6   3 oz. chicken breast
    1 cup noodles
    1/2 cup sauteed mushrooms
    1/2 cup asparagus
    1 cup skim milk

7   1/2 cup sugar-free vanilla pudding

8   2 plums or 1/2 cup your choice of canned
    fruit in own juice or water

# WEEK 2: WEDNESDAY

## 1000 Calories

1    1/2 cup Bran Flakes
     1 cup skim milk

2    1/2 grapefruit

3    2 oz. boiled ham
     2 slices whole wheat bread

4    1 tomato

5    Salad
          1/2 cup spinach
          1/3 cup celery
          1/3 cup mushrooms
     1 tbsp. fat-free dressing

6    2 oz. (baked) fish
     2/3 cup (cooked) rice
     1/2 cup cooked carrots
     1 cup skim milk

7    15 grapes

8    3 oz. non-fat frozen yogurt

# WEEK 2: THURSDAY

## 1000 Calories

| | |
|---|---|
| 1 | 1 bagel<br>1 tsp. diet jelly<br>1 cup skim milk |
| 2 | 1 orange |
| 3 | 1/2 cup raw cauliflower<br>1/2 cup raw broccoli<br>1 tbsp. fat-free dressing |
| 4 | 1/4 cup tuna<br>1/2 pita bread 6″ across<br>1 tsp. Miracle Whip (fat free)<br>6 saltine crackers |
| 5 | 3 medium prunes or 2 tbsp. raisins |
| 6 | 3 oz. pork tenderloin<br>1/2 cup corn<br>1 cup green beans |
| 7 | 8 oz. non-fat yogurt |
| 8 | 1/2 cup sugar-free vanilla pudding |

# WEEK 2: FRIDAY

## 1000 Calories

1    1/2 cup egg substitute
2 slices whole wheat toast
1 cup skim milk

2    1/2 grapefruit or 1/2 cup grapefruit juice

3    1 cup vegetable soup (see recipe)
6 saltine crackers

4    2/3 cup cottage cheese
1/3 cup pineapple chunks in water or
     own juice

5    3 cups (air popped) popcorn or microwave
popcorn with less than 2 grams of fat per
3 cups

6    1 medium baked potato
1/2 cup broccoli cooked
1 oz. fat-free cheese, melted over broccoli
     and potato
1/2 cup skim milk

7    6 graham crackers (2.5" square)
1/2 cup skim milk

8    1 serving sugar-free gelatin

# WEEK 2: SATURDAY

## 1000 Calories

1  2 pancakes (4″ across)
   3/4 cup blueberries
   1 tbsp. light syrup
   1 cup skim milk

2  1/2 cup fruit cocktail in own juice or water

3  4 oz. non-fat yogurt

4  1 bagel
   1 oz. fat-free cheese

5  Salad:
      1/2 cup lettuce,
      1/2 cup spinach,
      1/3 cup green pepper,
      1/3 cup alfalfa sprouts,
      1/3 cup radishes
   1 tbs. lemon juice

6  3 oz. lean sirloin beef
   1/2 cup peas
   1/2 cup corn
   1/2 cup skim milk

7  1 cup raw carrots

8  3/4 oz. pretzels

# WEEK 3

## Meats

Egg substitute
Healthy Choice hot dog
Lean beef sirloin
Tuna packed in water
Skinless chicken
Skinless turkey breast
Fish
Ham
Pork tenderloin
Shrimp

## Fruits

Orange
Peaches or canned
   peaches packed in
   own juice or water
Bananas
Prunes, raisins or
   plums
Orange juice
Apple
Fruit cocktail packed
   in own juice or
   water
Grapes
Grapefruit
Pineapple chunks
   packed in own juice
   or water
Strawberries (fresh or
   frozen)

## Breads/starches

Whole wheat bread
Vanilla wafers
Hot dog bun
Potatoes
Bran Flakes
Bagel
Rice
Graham crackers
Popcorn
Grapenuts
Pretzels
Whole wheat crackers
Pita bread (6″ across)
Noodles
Pancake mix (complete
   pancake mix or
   frozen pancakes
   with less than 2
   grams of fat)

## Vegetables

Sauerkraut
Mushrooms
Spinach
Celery
Lettuce
Cucumber
Beets
Carrots
Tomato
Green beans
Broccoli

Tomato juice
Brussels sprouts
Bean sprouts
Radishes

## Dairy products
Skim milk
Fat-free yogurt
Fat-free sour cream
Non-fat frozen yogurt
Low-fat cottage cheese
Parmesan cheese

## Miscellaneous condiments
Fat-free salad dressing
Pickles
Salsa
Mustard (Dijon)
Pickle relish
Sugar-free pudding
Miracle Whip (fat free)
 or mayonnaise
Diet jelly
Light syrup

# WEEK 3: SUNDAY

## 1000 Calories

1   1/2 cup Bran Flakes
    1/2 cup skim milk

2   1/2 bagel
    1/2 cup orange juice

3   1 cup celery sticks

4   1/4 cup tuna
    1/2 pita bread (6" across)
    1 tsp. Miracle Whip (fat free) (for tuna)
    1 pickle

5   Salad:
        1 cup lettuce
        1/2 cup cucumber
    1 tbsp. fat-free dressing

6   3 oz. chicken
    2/3 cup (cooked) rice
    1/2 cup beets
    1 cup skim milk

7   3 prunes or 2 tbsp. raisins or 2 plums

8   3 graham crackers (2.5" square)
    1/2 cup skim milk

# WEEK 3: MONDAY

## 1000 Calories

1    2 slices whole wheat toast
1 tsp. diet jelly
1 cup skim milk

2    1 cup carrot sticks

3    1 orange

4    2 oz. turkey breast
2 slices whole wheat bread
1 slice tomato

5    1/2 bagel
1/2 cup skim milk

6    2 oz. fish (baked or grilled)
1/2 cup green beans
1/2 cup broccoli

7    1 baked apple (see recipe)
1/2 cup skim milk

8    3 cups (air popped) popcorn or microwave
popcorn with 2 grams or less of fat
per 3 cups

# WEEK 3: TUESDAY

## 1000 Calories

1   1/2 cup Bran Flakes
    1/2 cup skim milk

2   4 oz. non-fat yogurt
    3 tbsp. Grapenuts
    1 small banana or 1/2 banana (9″)

3   1/2 cup tomato juice

4   2 oz. boiled ham
    2 slices whole wheat bread

5   1 pear or 1/2 cup canned pears in own
        juice or water

6   2 oz. lean sirloin beef
    1 medium baked potato
    1/2 cup green beans
    1 tbsp. fat-free sour cream
    1 cup skim milk

7   Salad:
        1 cup spinach
        1/2 cup mushrooms
    1 tbsp. fat-free dressing

8   3 oz. non-fat frozen yogurt
    1-1/4 cup strawberries

# WEEK 3: WEDNESDAY

## 1000 Calories

1   2 slices whole wheat toast
    1 cup skim milk

2   15 grapes

3   1 cup carrot sticks

4   1/4 cup tuna
    2 slices whole wheat bread
    1 tsp. mustard and 1 tsp. pickle relish
        mixed into tuna

5   6 whole wheat crackers
    2 tbsp. salsa

6   3 oz. chicken
    1 cup broccoli
    1 cup skim milk

7   1/2 cup fruit cocktail in its own juice or
    water

8   3/4 oz. pretzels

# WEEK 3: THURSDAY

## 1000 Calories

1   1/2 cup Bran Flakes
    1/2 cup skim milk

2   1/2 grapefruit or 1/2 cup grapefruit juice

3   1 cup celery sticks

4   Vegetarian pita (see recipe)

5   1/2 cup low-fat cottage cheese
    1/3 cup pineapple chunks in own juice
      or water

6   2 oz. pork tenderloin
    1 cup noodles
    1/2 cup brussels sprouts
    1 cup skim milk

7   1/2 cup sugar-free vanilla pudding

8   1/2 bagel
    1/2 cup skim milk

# WEEK 3: FRIDAY

## 1000 Calories

1   2 pancakes (4" across)
    1 tbsp. light syrup
    1 cup skim milk

2   1/2 cup orange juice

3   1 cup vegetable soup (see recipe)
    6 saltine crackers

4   1 oz. chicken
    2/3 cup (cooked) rice with 1/2 cup cooked
      celery

5   15 grapes

6   2 oz. steamed shrimp
    1/2 cup noodles
    1/3 cup parmesan cheese

7   Salad:
        1 cup lettuce
        1/2 cup cucumber
        1/4 cup radishes
    1 tbsp. fat-free dressing

8   3 graham crackers (2.5" square)
    1 cup skim milk

# WEEK 3: SATURDAY

## 1000 Calories

1   1/2 cup egg substitute
    1 slice whole wheat toast
    1 cup skim milk

2   1 orange

3   6 vanilla wafers
    1/2 cup skim milk

4   1 Healthy Choice hot dog
    1 hot dog bun
    1/2 cup sauerkraut

5   1 peach or 1/2 cup canned peaches in
        water or own juice

6   3 oz. lean sirloin beef
    1/2 cup sauteed mushrooms
    1/2 cup cooked spinach
    1 cup mashed potatoes

7   1 small banana or 1/2 banana (9")

8   4 oz. non-fat yogurt

# WEEK 4

## Meats
- Skinless chicken breast
- Turkey
- Tuna packed in water
- Fish
- Ham
- Healthy Choice hot dog
- Flank steak

## Fruits
- Orange juice
- Strawberries (if not in season, substitute choice of canned fruit in own juice or in water or frozen strawberries)
- Pineapple chunks packed in own juice or water
- Grapes
- Banana
- Cantaloupe
- Pear
- Apple

## Bread/Starches
- Pancake mix (complete pancake mix or frozen pancakes with less than 2 grams of fat)
- Rice (white)
- Pretzels
- Whole wheat bread
- Potatoes
- Bagels
- English muffin
- Pita bread
- Popcorn
- Graham crackers
- Bran Flakes
- Bread sticks
- Noodles
- Hot dog bun
- Vanilla wafers
- Flour tortilla shells (7 inch)

## Vegetables
- Lettuce
- Celery
- Green onions
- Carrots
- Asparagus
- Tomato juice
- Broccoli
- Zucchini
- Bean sprouts
- Mushrooms
- Tomato
- Canned tomatoes
- Green beans
- Cucumber
- Green pepper
- Brussels sprouts

Dairy products
  Skim milk
  Low-fat cottage cheese
  Fat-free yogurt
  Fat-free cheese
  Non-fat frozen yogurt

Miscellaneous/
condiments
  Light syrup

Lemon juice
Diet pop
Sugar-free gelatin
Diet jelly
Salsa
Honey
Weight Watchers Smart
  One Lemon Herb
  Chicken

## WEEK 4: SUNDAY

## 1000 Calories

1   2 slices whole wheat toast
    1 tsp. diet jelly
    1 cup skim milk

2   1/2 cup orange juice

3   2 oz. sliced turkey
    2 slices whole wheat bread
    1 cup celery sticks

4   1/3 cup pineapple chunks in own juice or
    water

5   1/2 cup tomato juice

6   1 medium baked potato
    2 oz. fat-free cheese, melted over broccoli
    and potato
    1/2 cup broccoli

7   1/2 bagel
    1 cup skim milk

8   1/2 cup sugar-free gelatin

# WEEK 4: MONDAY

## 1000 Calories

1    2 slices whole wheat toast
      1 cup skim milk

2    1 bagel
      1 oz. fat-free cheese

3    Salad:
         1 cup lettuce
         1/4 cup green onions
         1/4 cup zucchini
      1 tbsp. lemon juice

4    1/2 grapefruit or 1/2 cup grapefruit juice

5    Weight Watchers Smart One Lemon
        Herb Chicken
      1 cup skim milk

6    1/4 cup low-fat cottage cheese

7    8 tortilla chips (see recipe)
      2 tbsp. salsa
      Diet pop

8    15 grapes

## WEEK 4:  TUESDAY

## 1000 Calories

1    1/2 English muffin
     1 tsp. honey
     1/2 cup orange juice
     1/2 cup skim milk

2    4 oz. non-fat yogurt

3    2 oz. Healthy Choice Chicken
     1 pita bread
     1/2 cup bean sprouts
     2 slices tomato

4    1 cucumber

5    2 oz. ground sirloin
     1 hamburger bun
     1/2 cup beets
     1 cup skim milk

6    1 cup vegetable soup (see recipe)

7    1 small banana or 1/2 banana (9″)

8    3 cups (air popped) popcorn or microwave
     popcorn with less than 2 grams of fat per
     3 cups

# WEEK 4:  WEDNESDAY

## 1000 Calories

1    1 slice whole wheat toast
     1/3 cantaloupe
     1 cup skim milk

2    1/2 cup carrot sticks
     1/2 cup celery sticks

3    1/4 cup tuna
     1 bagel
     1 tsp. Miracle Whip (fat free)

4    3 graham crackers (2.5″ square)
     1/2 cup skim milk

5    3 oz. fish (baked or grilled)
     2/3 cup (cooked) rice
     1/2 cup pea pods

6    Salad:
          1 cup lettuce
          1/2 cup mushrooms
          1/2 cup cucumber
     1 tbsp. fat-free dressing

7    1 cup fat-free yogurt

8    1 pear

# WEEK 4: THURSDAY

## 1000 Calories

1   1/2 cup Bran Flakes
    1 cup skim milk

2   1/2 cup orange juice

3   1 oz. ham
    1 slice whole wheat bread
    1 tomato
    Lettuce

4   1 cup vegetable soup (see recipe)
    2 bread sticks (crisp)

5   1 cup skim milk

6   3 oz. turkey breast
    1/2 cup green beans
    1/2 cup noodles

7   1 baked apple (see recipe)

8   3 oz. non-fat frozen yogurt

## WEEK 4: FRIDAY

### 1000 Calories

1   1/2 cup egg substitute
    1 slice whole wheat toast
    1 tsp. diet jelly
    1 cup skim milk

2   1/2 cup grapefruit or 1/2 cup
        grapefruit juice

3   1 Healthy Choice hot dog
    1 hot dog bun
    1/2 cup brussels sprouts

4   1/2 cup low-fat pudding

5   1/2 cup tomato juice

6   3 oz. flank steak
    1 serving steak fries (see recipe)
    1/2 cup steamed broccoli

7   1 small banana or 1/2 banana (9")

8   6 vanilla wafers
    1 cup skim milk

# WEEK 4:  SATURDAY

## 1000 Calories

1   2 pancakes (4″ across)
1 tbsp. light syrup
1 cup skim milk

2   1/2 cup orange juice

3   1/2 cup cottage cheese
1-1/4 cup strawberries

4   Salad:
1 cup lettuce
1/4 cup celery
1/4 cup green onions

5   1 bagel
1/2 cup skim milk

6   2 oz. chicken breast
2/3 cup (cooked) rice
1/2 cup asparagus

7   4 oz. non-fat yogurt

8   3/4 oz. pretzels
Diet pop

# VI

# 1200 CALORIES
## SHOPPING LIST AND MENUS

## WEEK 1

### Meats
Egg substitute
Turkey breast
Shrimp
Pork tenderloin
Ground sirloin
Fish
Healthy Choice hot
    dog
Tuna packed in water
Ham
Beef tenderloin

### Fruits
Orange juice
Grapes
Pears
Plum
Grapefruit or grapefruit
    juice

Apples
Banana
Pineapple chunks
    packed in own juice
    or water
Fruit cocktail packed
    in own juice or
    water
Oranges
Strawberries, fresh or
    frozen
Fruit juice—100%
    juice, no additions
    such as high
    fructose corn syrup;
    should state "juice
    from concentrate"
    (good choices are
    Juicy Juice or Motts)
Peach or canned

peaches in own
juice or water
Cantaloupe
Kiwi

Breads/starches
Oatmeal
Whole wheat bread
Rice (white or brown)
Bagels
Whole-grain English
muffins
Potatoes
Grapenuts
Bran Flakes
Pita bread (6″ across)
Popcorn
Saltine crackers
Hamburger bun
Graham crackers
Pancake mix (complete
pancake mix or
frozen pancakes
with less than 2
grams of fat)
Hot dog bun
Noodles

Vegetables
Lettuce
Mushrooms
Green pepper
Onion
Pea pods

Spinach
Tomato juice
Carrots
Celery
Tomato
Alfalfa sprouts
Cucumbers
Broccoli
Beets
Sauerkraut
Cauliflower
Green beans

Dairy
Skim milk
Non-fat yogurt
Margarine or diet
margarine
Fat-free cheese
Low-fat cottage cheese
Non-fat frozen yogurt

Miscellaneous/
condiments
Sunflower seeds
Fat-free salad dressing
Pickles
Miracle Whip (fat free)
or mayonnaise
Diet jam or jelly
Sugar-free gelatin
Diet syrup

# WEEK 1: SUNDAY

## 1200 Calories

1    1/2 cup (cooked) oatmeal
1 cup skim milk
1/2 cup orange juice

2    15 grapes

3    2 oz. turkey breast
2 slices whole wheat bread

4    1 pear

5    Salad:
        1 cup lettuce
        1/2 cup mushrooms
        1/4 cup green peppers
        1/4 cup onions
        1 tbsp. sunflower seeds
1 tbsp. fat-free dressing

6    2 oz. shrimp
1 cup pea pods
2/3 cup (cooked) rice

7    1 plum or 1/2 cup canned fruit in own
juice or water

8    1/2 bagel
1 cup skim milk

# WEEK 1: MONDAY

## 1200 Calories

1    1 wheat grain English muffin
1 cup skim milk
1 tbsp. diet margarine

2    1/2 grapefruit or 1/2 cup grapefruit juice

3    2 oz. fat-free cheese
1 bagel

4    1 apple

5    1/2 cup tomato juice (low-sodium
preferred)

6    2 oz. pork tenderloin
1 medium baked potato
1 cup spinach

7    8 oz. nonfat yogurt
3 tbsp. Grapenuts

8    1 banana (9")

# WEEK 1: TUESDAY

## 1200 Calories

1    1/2 cup Bran Flakes
     1 cup skim milk
     1/2 cup egg substitute

2    2/3 cup pineapple chunks in own juice
        or in water

3    1/2 cup tuna
     1 pita bread (6″ across)
     1 pickle
     Lettuce
     1 tbsp. Miracle Whip (fat free)

4    1 cup carrot sticks
     1 cup celery sticks
     1 tbsp. fat-free dressing

5    1/2 cup fruit cocktail in own juice or in
        water

6    Weight Watchers Lemon Herb
        Chicken Piccata
     1 cup skim milk

7    1 orange

8    3 cups (air popped) popcorn or microwave
        popcorn with 2 grams of fat or less in
        3 cups

# WEEK 1:  WEDNESDAY

## 1200 Calories

1    2 slices whole wheat toast
1 cup skim milk
1 tsp. margarine or 1 tbsp. diet margarine

2    1/2 grapefruit or 1/2 cup grapefruit juice

3    1/2 cup low-fat cottage cheese
1-1/4 cup strawberries

4    6 saltine crackers

5    Salad:
        1 cup lettuce
        1/2 tomato
        1/4 cup celery
        1/4 cup alfalfa sprouts
        1/4 cup cucumbers
1 tbsp. fat-free dressing

6    2 oz. ground round hamburger
1 hamburger bun
1 cup broccoli
1 pickle
1 cup skim milk

7    30 grapes

8    3 oz. nonfat frozen yogurt

# WEEK 1: THURSDAY

## 1200 Calories

1    1/2 cup egg substitute
1 whole grain English muffin
1 cup skim milk
1 tbsp. diet jelly or jam

2    1 orange

3    Vegetarian pita (see recipe for 1200-calorie pita)

4    1 cup fruit juice

5    3 graham crackers (2.5" square)
1 cup skim milk

6    3 oz. lean turkey
1 medium baked potato
1/2 cup beets
1 tsp. margarine or 1 tbsp. diet margarine

7    1 pear

8    1/2 cup sugar-free gelatin

# WEEK 1: FRIDAY

## 1200 Calories

1   2 pancakes (4″ across)
    1/2 cup blueberries
    1/2 cup orange juice
    1 cup skim milk
    1 tbsp. diet syrup

2   1/2 cup celery sticks
    1/2 cup carrot sticks
    1 tbsp. fat-free dressing

3   1 Healthy Choice hot dog
    1 hot dog bun
    1/2 cup sauerkraut
    1/2 cup skim milk

4   1 peach or 1/2 cup canned peaches in own
    juice or water

5   Salad:
        1 lettuce
        1/2 cup cauliflower
        1/2 cup mushrooms
    1 tbsp. fat-free dressing

6   3 oz. fish
    2/3 cup (cooked) rice
    1/2 cup peas
    1/2 cup skim milk

7   1 baked apple (see recipe)

8   3 cups (air-popped) popcorn or microwave
    popcorn with less than 2 grams of fat per
    3 cups

# WEEK 1: SATURDAY

## 1200 Calories

1    2 slices whole wheat toast
1 cup skim milk
1 tsp. margarine or 1 tbsp. diet margarine

2    1/2 cantaloupe

3    2 oz. sliced ham
1 slice whole wheat toast
Tomato slices
Lettuce

4    1 banana (9")

5    3 graham crackers (2-1/2" square)
1/2 cup skim milk

6    2 oz. beef tenderloin
1 cup noodles
1 cup green beans
1 tsp. margarine

7    1/2 cup tomato juice

8    4 oz. nonfat plain yogurt
2 large kiwi

# WEEK 2

Meats
- Turkey
- Chicken breast
- Ham
- Fish
- Tuna packed in water
- Healthy Choice hot dog

Fruits
- Raisins
- Orange juice
- Watermelon (If not in season, may substitute 1/2 c. canned fruit packed in its own juice or in water)
- Cantaloupe
- Apples
- Kiwi
- Nectarine
- Grapes
- Pear
- Oranges
- Peach or canned peaches packed in own juice or in water
- Plums
- Grapefruit
- Strawberries, fresh or frozen
- Pineapple chunks canned in own juice or in water
- Fruit cocktail packed in its own juice or in water
- Banana
- Prunes
- Apple juice

Breads/starches
- Bran Flakes
- Whole wheat bread
- Rice (white or brown)
- Bagels
- Popcorn
- English muffins
- Graham crackers
- Potato
- Grapenuts
- Pancake mix (complete pancake mix or frozen pancakes with less than 2 grams of fat)
- Hot dog bun
- Saltine crackers
- Flour tortilla shells (7 inch)

Vegetables
- Celery
- Cauliflower
- Broccoli
- Carrots
- Lettuce
- Spinach

Radish
Mushrooms
Green beans
Tomato
Asparagus
Zucchini
Corn
Pimentos
Sauerkraut

## Dairy

Skim milk
Non-fat yogurt
Low-fat cottage cheese
Non-fat frozen yogurt
Fat-free cheese
Margarine or diet
   margarine

## Miscellaneous/ condiments

Salsa
Miracle Whip (fat free)
   or mayonnaise
Fat-free salad dressing
Sugar-free pudding
Diet jam or jelly
Budget Light Oriental
   Beef frozen entree
Sugar-free gelatin
Budget Light Sirloin of
   Beef in Herb Sauce
   frozen entree
Diet syrup

# WEEK 2: SUNDAY

## 1200 Calories

1. 1/2 cup Bran Flakes
   2 tbsp. raisins
   1 cup skim milk

2. 1 cup orange juice

3. 2 oz. turkey
   1 slice whole wheat bread
   1 tbsp. Miracle Whip (fat free)

4. 1 cup celery sticks
   1 cup cauliflower florets
   1 tbsp. fat-free dressing

5. 1-1/4 cup watermelon cubes or 1/2 cup
   canned fruit in juice or water

6. 2 oz. skinless chicken breast
   2/3 cup (cooked) rice
   1/2 cup broccoli
   1 tsp. margarine or 1 tbsp. diet margarine

7. 8 oz. nonfat yogurt
   3 tbsp. Grapenuts

8. 1/2 cup fat-free pudding

# WEEK 2: MONDAY

## 1200 Calories

1   1 slice whole wheat toast
    1 tsp. jam/jelly
    1/3 cantaloupe
    1 cup skim milk

2   1 cup carrot sticks

3   2 oz. ham
    1 bagel
    1 apple

4   1 kiwi
    1/4 cup low-fat cottage cheese

5   Salad:
        1 cup lettuce
        1/2 cup spinach
        1/4 cup radish
        1/4 cup mushrooms
    1 tbsp. fat-free dressing

6   Budget Light Oriental Beef
    1 cup skim milk

7   1 nectarine or orange

8   3 cups (air popped) popcorn or microwave
    with less than 2 grams of fat per 3 cups

# WEEK 2: TUESDAY

## 1200 Calories

1  1 English muffin
   1 cup skim milk
   1 cup orange juice
   1 tsp. margarine or 1 tbsp. diet margarine

2  15 grapes

3  2 oz. chicken
   2 slices whole wheat bread
   Tomato slice
   Lettuce
   1 cucumber
   1 tsp. Miracle Whip (fat free)

4  8 oz. nonfat yogurt

5  Salad:
      1 cup lettuce
      1/4 cup celery
      1/2 cup cauliflower
      1/2 cup broccoli
   1 tbsp. fat-free dressing

6  Grilled Cheese: 2 oz. fat-free cheese,
      2 slices whole wheat bread (see recipe)
   1/2 cup green beans
   1 pickle

7  1 pear

8  1/2 cup sugar-free gelatin

# WEEK 2:  WEDNESDAY

## 1200 Calories

1    1/2 cup Bran Flakes
1/2 cup apple juice
1 cup skim milk

2    1 orange

3    1/2 cup tuna
1 bagel
1 slice tomato
Lettuce
1 cup carrot sticks
1 pickle
1 tsp. Miracle Whip (fat free)

4    2 small plums

5    3 graham crackers (2.5")
1/2 cup skim milk

6    2 oz. fish
2/3 cup (cooked) rice
1/2 cup asparagus
1/2 cup carrots
1 tsp. margarine

7    1/2 cup fat-free yogurt

8    1 peach or 1/2 cup canned peaches in
juice or water

# WEEK 2: THURSDAY

## 1200 Calories

1    1 slice whole wheat toast
     1 cup skim milk
     1 tsp. diet jelly/jam

2    1 grapefruit or 1 cup grapefruit juice

3    2 oz. turkey
     1 slice whole wheat bread
     1 tbsp. Miracle Whip (fat free)

4    1 apple

5    Salad:
         1 cup spinach
         1/2 cup mushrooms
         1/4 cup celery
         1/4 cup radish
     1 tbsp. fat-free dressing
     2 bread sticks

6    1 medium baked potato
     2 oz. fat-free cheese, melted over broccoli
         and potato
     1 cup broccoli
     1 cup skim milk

7    1/2 cup nonfat frozen yogurt
     1-1/4 cup whole strawberries

8    8 tortilla chips (see recipe)
     1 tbsp. salsa

# WEEK 2: FRIDAY

## 1200 Calories

1. 1/2 cup egg substitute
   2 slices whole wheat toast
   1 cup skim milk
   1/2 cup orange juice

2. 1/2 cup fat-free yogurt
   3 tbsp. Grapenuts

3. 1/4 cup low-fat cottage cheese
   1/3 cup pineapple chunks in own juice
     or water

4. Mixed vegetables:
   1/2 cup zucchini
   1/2 cup corn
   1/3 cup pimentos

5. 15 grapes

6. Budget Gourmet Light Sirloin of Beef in
     Herb Sauce
   1 diced tomato
   1/2 cup skim milk

7. 1/2 cup fruit cocktail in own juice or water

8. 3 graham crackers (2.5" square)
   1/2 cup skim milk

# WEEK 2: SATURDAY

## 1200 Calories

1   2 pancakes (4" across)
    1 cup skim milk
    1 tbsp. diet syrup

2   1 orange

3   1 Healthy Choice hot dog
    1 hot dog bun
    1/2 cup sauerkraut

4   Salad:
        1 cup lettuce
        1/2 cup spinach
        1/2 cup cauliflower
        1/2 cup diced tomato
    1 tbsp. fat-free dressing

5   1 banana (9")

6   2 oz. ham
    1 cup mashed potatoes
    1 tsp. margarine or 1 tbsp. diet margarine
    1/2 cup green beans
    1 cup skim milk

7   1 oz. fat-free cheese
    6 saltine crackers

8   3 prunes or 2 tbsp. raisins or 2 plums

# WEEK 3

## Meats

- Tuna packed in water
- Turkey
- Ham
- Shrimp
- Ground sirloin hamburger
- Pork tenderloin
- Fish
- Egg substitute

## Fruits

- Raisins
- Cantaloupe
- Peaches or canned peaches in own juice or water
- Raspberries (If not in season may substitute canned fruit packed in its own juice or in water)
- Apple juice
- Plums
- Orange
- Fruit cocktail packed in own juice or in water
- Orange juice
- Pear
- Blueberries, fresh or frozen
- Bananas
- Applesauce
- Fruit juice
- Prunes
- Strawberries, fresh or frozen
- Grapes
- Pineapple chunks packed in own juice or in water
- Apple

## Breads/starches

- Bran Flakes
- Pita bread (6" across)
- Stuffing
- Popcorn
- Oatmeal
- Whole wheat bread
- Vanilla wafers
- Rice (white or brown)
- Whole-grain English muffin
- Pretzels
- Graham crackers
- Noodles
- Bagel
- Pancake mix (complete pancake mix or frozen pancakes with less than 2 grams of fat)
- Bread sticks

Flour tortilla shells (7 inches)

## Vegetables

Lettuce
Celery
Carrots
Beets
Brussels sprouts
Broccoli
Mixed vegetables
Spinach
Mushrooms
Cucumber
Tomato
Alfalfa sprouts
Water chestnuts
Tomato juice
Radishes
Peas
Cauliflower
Green beans

## Dairy

Skim milk
Non-fat yogurt
Fat-free shredded cheddar cheese
Non-fat frozen yogurt
Low-fat cottage cheese
Margarine or diet margarine
Fat-free cream cheese

## Miscellaneous/condiments

Fat-free salad dressing
Diet jam or jelly
Sugar-free gelatin
Stouffer's Lean Cuisine Breast of Chicken Parmesan
Diet syrup
Salsa

# WEEK 3: SUNDAY

## 1200 Calories

1    1/2 cup Bran Flakes
     2 tbsp. raisins
     1 cup skim milk

2    1/3 cantaloupe

3    1/2 cup tuna
     1 pita bread (6" across)
     Lettuce
     1/2 tbsp. Miracle Whip (fat free)

4    1/2 cup carrot sticks
     1/2 cup celery sticks

5    1 peach or 1/2 cup canned peaches in own
        juice or water

6    1 oz. turkey
     1 cup stuffing
     1/2 cup beets
     1/2 cup brussel sprouts
     1/2 cup skim milk

7    4 oz. non-fat yogurt
     1 cup raspberries or 1/2 cup canned fruit
        in own juice or water

8    3 cups (air popped) popcorn or microwave
        popcorn with 2 grams fat or less per 3
        cups

# WEEK 3: MONDAY

## 1200 Calories

1   1/2 cup oatmeal
    1/2 cup apple juice
    1/2 cup skim milk

2   2 plums

3   2 oz. sliced ham
    1 slice whole wheat bread
    1 cup raw broccoli
    1 tomato
    1 tbsp. fat-free dressing

4   6 vanilla wafers
    1 cup skim milk

5   1 orange

6   1 oz. shrimp
    2/3 cup (cooked) rice
    1/2 cup mixed vegetables
    1 tsp. margarine or 1 tbsp. diet margarine

7   1/2 cup fruit cocktail in its own juice or
       water

8   1 slice whole wheat toast
    1/2 cup skim milk
    1 tsp. diet jam or jelly

# WEEK 3: TUESDAY

## 1200 Calories

1     1 whole-grain English muffin
       1 cup skim milk
       1/2 cup orange juice
       1 tsp. margarine or 1 tbsp. diet margarine
       1 tsp. diet jelly

2     15 grapes

3     Salad:
           1 oz. turkey (cut into strips)
           1 cup lettuce
           1/4 cup water chestnuts
           1/2 cup spinach
           1/4 cup mushrooms
           1/4 cup cucumber
       1 tbsp. fat-free dressing
       1 cup skim milk

4     3/4 oz. pretzels

5     1 pear

6     2 oz. ground sirloin hamburger
       2 soft tortilla shells (6" across)
       2 tbsp. salsa
       1/4 cup green onion
       1 oz. fat-free shredded cheddar cheese
       diced tomato
       1/2 cup shredded lettuce

7     3 oz. non-fat frozen yogurt
       1/4 cup blueberries

8     1/2 cup sugar-free gelatin

# WEEK 3: WEDNESDAY

## 1200 Calories

1    2 slices whole wheat toast
1 cup skim milk
1 tsp. diet jelly or jam
1 tsp. margarine or 1 tbsp. diet margarine

2    1 banana (9″)

3    Vegetarian pita (see recipe)

4    1/4 cup low-fat cottage cheese
1/3 cantaloupe

5    3 graham crackers (2.5″ square)

6    3 oz. pork tenderloin
1/2 cup noodles
1/2 cup spinach
1/2 cup water chestnuts
1/2 cup skim milk

7    1/2 cup applesauce

8    4 oz. fat-free yogurt

# WEEK 3: THURSDAY

## 1200 Calories

1   1/2 cup Bran Flakes
    1 cup skim milk
    1/2 cup orange juice

2   1 peach or 1/2 cup canned peaches in own
    juice or water

3   1 bagel
    2 tbsp. fat-free cream cheese
    1/2 cup celery sticks
    1/3 cup carrot sticks

4   6 vanilla wafers
    1/2 cup skim milk

5   1/2 cup fruit cocktail in own juice or in
    water

6   Stouffer's Lean Cuisine Breast of Chicken
    Parmesan
    1/2 cup skim milk

7   3 medium prunes or 2 tbsp. raisins or 2
    plums

8   1/2 cup sugar-free pudding

# WEEK 3: FRIDAY

## 1200 Calories

1  2 pancakes (4″ across)
   1-1/4 cup strawberries or 3/4 cup frozen
      blueberries
   1 cup skim milk
   Diet syrup

2  1/2 cup tomato juice

3  1/3 cup cantaloupe

4  Salad:
       1 cup lettuce
       1/4 cup tuna
       1/2 cup cucumber slices
       1/4 cup radishes
   2 bread sticks
   1 tbsp. fat-free dressing

5  15 grapes

6  3 oz. fish
   2/3 cup (cooked) rice
   1/2 cup carrots
   1/2 cup peas
   1 cup skim milk

7  1/2 cup sugar-free gelatin

8  3 oz. fat-free frozen yogurt
   1/3 cup pineapple chunks in own juice or
      water

# WEEK 3: SATURDAY

## 1200 Calories

1   1/2 cup egg substitute
1 whole-grain English muffin
1 cup skim milk
1 tsp. margarine or 1 tbsp. diet margarine

2   1 apple

3   1/4 cup low-fat cottage cheese
1 orange

4   1/2 bagel
1/2 cup skim milk

5   Salad:
     1 cup spinach
     1/4 cup mushroom
     1/2 cup celery
     1/4 cup cauliflower
1 tbsp. fat-free dressing

6   2 oz. ground sirloin hamburger
1/2 cup spaghetti sauce
1 cup spaghetti noodles
1/2 cup green beans
1/2 cup skim milk

7   1 banana (9")

8   8 tortilla chips (see recipe)
1 tbsp. salsa

# WEEK 4

## Meats

- Ham
- Turkey
- Pork tenderloin
- Tuna
- Chicken breast
- Fish
- Beef tenderloin
- Egg substitute
- Healthy Choice hot dog
- Cornish hen

## Fruits

- Orange
- Pineapple chunks packed in own juice or in water
- Pear
- Grapefruit or grapefruit juice
- Raisins
- Peaches or canned peaches in own juice or in water
- Orange juice
- Grapes
- Banana
- Applesauce
- Plums
- Fruit cocktail packed in own juice or in water
- Fruit juice
- Kiwi
- Strawberries, fresh or frozen
- Blueberries, fresh or frozen

## Breads/starches

- Bran Flakes
- Whole wheat bread
- Potatoes
- Popcorn
- Bagels
- Graham crackers
- Pita (6" across)
- Soft frozen pretzel
- English muffin
- Rice (white or brown)
- Vanilla wafers
- Bread sticks
- Pancake mix (complete pancake mix or frozen pancakes with less than 2 grams of fat)
- Hot dog buns

## Vegetables

- Lettuce
- Tomato
- Carrots
- Tomato juice
- Corn
- Broccoli
- Canned tomatoes

Green onions
Green pepper
Cucumber
Alfalfa sprouts
Peas
Celery
Zucchini
Mushrooms
Spinach
Beets
Cauliflower
Radish
Onion
Sauerkraut
Red cabbage
Water chestnuts
Green beans

## Dairy
Skim milk

Low-fat cottage cheese
Fat-free frozen yogurt
Fat-free cream cheese
Margarine or diet
 margarine

## Miscellaneous/ condiments
Weight Watchers Smart
 One Lasagna
 Florentine
Peanuts
Sugar-free gelatin
Miracle Whip (fat free)
 or mayonnaise
Fat-free salad dressing
Diet syrup

# WEEK 4: SUNDAY

## 1200 Calories

1    1/2 cup Bran Flakes
1 cup skim milk

2    1 orange

3    2 oz. sliced ham
2 slices whole wheat bread
1 slice tomato
Lettuce
1 cup carrot sticks
1/2 cup skim milk

4    2/3 cup pineapple chunks in own juice or
water

5    1/2 cup tomato juice

6    2 oz. turkey breast
1/2 cup corn
1/2 cup mashed potatoes
1/2 cup broccoli
1/2 cup skim milk
1 tsp. margarine or tbsp. diet margarine

7    1 pear

8    3 cups (air popped) popcorn or microwave
with less than 2 grams of fat per 3 cups

# WEEK 4: MONDAY

## 1200 Calories

1    2 slices whole wheat toast
1 cup skim milk
1 tsp. diet jelly

2    1/2 grapefruit or 1/2 cup grapefruit juice

3    1/2 cup low-fat cottage cheese
1/2 cup canned peaches in own juice or
    water
1 bagel

4    3 graham crackers (2.5" square)
1/2 cup skim milk

5    1 cup vegetable soup (see recipe)

6    Weight Watchers Smart One Lasagna
    Florentine
1/2 cup skim milk

7    4 tbsp. raisins
20 peanuts

8    1 cup sugar-free gelatin

# WEEK 4: TUESDAY

## 1200 Calories

1   1/2 cup Bran Flakes
    1 cup skim milk

2   1/2 cup orange juice

3   Vegetarian Pita (see recipe)

4   15 grapes

5   1 medium baked potato
    2 oz. melted fat-free cheese
    1/2 cup broccoli
    1/2 cup skim milk

6   2 oz. pork tenderloin
    1/2 cup peas
    1/2 cup carrots
    1/2 cup skim milk

7   1 banana (9")

8   1 soft frozen pretzel

# WEEK 4: WEDNESDAY

## 1200 Calories

1   1 English muffin
    1 cup skim milk
    1 tsp. margarine or 1 tbsp. diet margarine

2   2 plums

3   1/2 cup tuna
    1/2 bagel
    Lettuce
    1 tsp. Miracle Whip (fat free)

4   1/2 cup fruit cocktail packed in water or
    own juice

5   1 cup celery sticks

6   2 oz. skinless chicken breast
    2/3 cup (cooked) rice
    1/2 cup zucchini
    1/2 cup mushrooms
    1 cup skim milk

7   1/2 cup applesauce

8   1/2 cup fruit juice
    1 slice whole wheat toast
    1 tsp. diet jelly

# WEEK 4: THURSDAY

## 1200 calories

1    1/2 cup Bran Flakes
1 cup skim milk
1/2 cup orange juice

2    1 pear

3    2 oz. sliced turkey
2 slices whole wheat bread
1 tbsp. fat-free miracle whip
1 large tomato and 1 large cucumber sliced
    with 1 tbsp. fat-free Italian dressing

4    6 vanilla wafers
1/2 cup skim milk

5    Salad:
    1 cup spinach
    1/4 cup mushrooms
    1/4 cup radish
    1/2 cup cauliflower
1 tbsp. fat-free dressing

6    2 oz. fish
1 serving oven fries (see recipe)
1/2 cup beets
1/2 cup skim milk
1 tsp. margarine or 1 tbsp. diet margarine

7    30 grapes

8    3 oz. cup non-fat frozen yogurt

# WEEK 4: FRIDAY

## 1200 Calories

1    1/2 cup egg substitute
1 slice whole wheat toast
1/2 cup fruit juice
1 cup skim milk

2    1/2 grapefruit or 1/2 cup grapefruit juice

3    Salad:
      1 cup lettuce
      1/4 cup celery
      1/4 cup onion
1 tbsp. fat-free dressing

4    1 bagel
2 tbsp. fat-free cream cheese
1/2 cup skim milk

5    1 cup vegetable soup (see recipe)
2 bread sticks

6    3 oz. beef tenderloin
1/2 cup brussels sprouts
1/2 cup noodles
1/2 cup skim milk

7    Fruit cup:
      1 kiwi,
      1-1/4 cup whole strawberries (sliced).
May substitute 1 9-inch banana.

8    1/2 cup sugar-free pudding

# WEEK 4: SATURDAY

## 1200 Calories

1   2 pancakes (4″ across)
3/4 cup blueberries
1 cup skim milk
Diet syrup

2   1/2 cup orange juice

3   1 Healthy Choice hot dog
1 hot dog bun
1/2 cup sauerkraut
1/2 cup skim milk

4   Salad:
1 cup spinach
1/2 cup red cabbage (shredded)
1/4 cup water chestnuts
1/2 cup tomato (sliced)
1 tbsp. fat-free dressing

5   1 cup sugar-free gelatin mixed with
1/2 cup fruit cocktail

6   3 oz. cornish hen (without skin)
2/3 cup (cooked) rice
1/2 cup green beans

7   6 vanilla wafers
1/2 cup skim milk

8   1 peach or 1/2 cup canned peaches in its
own juice or water

# VII

# 1500 CALORIES
## SHOPPING LIST AND MENUS

## WEEK 1

Meats
> Tuna packed in water
> Ground sirloin
> > hamburger
> Turkey breast
> Ham
> Skinless chicken breast
> Flank steak
> Fish
> Egg substitute

Fruits
> Fruit cocktail packed
> > in own juice or in
> > water
> Orange juice
> Plums
> Peaches or canned
> > peaches in own
> > juice or in water

Fruit juice
Grapefruit
Grapes
Raisins
Apple juice
Cantaloupes
Apple
Watermelon (If not in
> season may
> substitute 1/2 c.
> canned fruit packe
> din own juice or in
> water)
Orange
Pineapple chunks
> packed in own juice
> or in water
Plums

Bread/starches
   Bran Flakes
   Whole wheat bread
   Pita bread
   Graham crackers
   Hamburger bun
   Potato
   Pretzels
   Vanilla wafers
   Rice (white or brown)
   Popcorn
   Bread sticks
   Saltine crackers
   Soft frozen pretzel
   Grapenuts
   Noodles

Vegetables
   Tomato juice
   Green beans
   Carrots
   Celery
   Peas
   Beets
   Lettuce
   Cucumber
   Alfalfa sprouts
   Broccoli
   Mushrooms
   Tomato
   Radishes
   Cauliflower
   Corn
   Spinach
   Canned tomatoes
   Green onion
   Green pepper

Dairy
   Skim milk
   Fat-free yogurt
   Non-fat frozen yogurt
   Fat-free sour cream
   Parmesan cheese
   Fat-free cheese
   Margarine or diet
      margarine

Miscellaneous/
condiments
   Miracle Whip (fat free)
      or mayonnaise
   Diet jam or jelly
   Sunflower seeds
   Molly McButter
   Pickles
   Fat-free dressing
   Light syrup

# WEEK 1: SUNDAY

## 1500 Calories

1  4 pancakes (4" across)
   2 tbsp. light syrup
   1 cup skim milk

2  1/3 cup cantaloupe

3  1 cup vegetable soup (see recipe)
   12 saltine crackers

4  1/2 cup low-fat cottage cheese
   1/2 cup canned peaches in its own juice or
      water or 1 peach

5  1 baked potato
   1/2 cup steamed broccoli
   1 tsp. fat-free sour cream

6  3 oz. chicken breast
   1 cup noodles
   1/2 cup spinach
   1 cup skim milk
   1 tsp. margarine or 1 tbsp. margarine

7  1/2 cup tomato juice

8  6 oz. frozen non-fat yogurt
   1/3 cup pineapple chunks packed in own
      juice or in water

# WEEK 1: MONDAY

## 1500 Calories

1    1/2 cup Bran Flakes
2 slices whole wheat toast
1/2 cup skim milk
1 tsp. margarine or 1 tbsp. diet margarine

2    1/2 cup orange juice

3    1/2 cup tuna
1 tsp. Miracle Whip (fat free)
1 pita bread
1 cup tomato juice

4    1 pear

5    3 graham crackers (2.5" square)
1/2 cup skim milk

6    3 oz. ground sirloin hamburger
1 hamburger bun
1 serving steak fries (see recipe)
1 cup green beans

7    8 oz. fat-free yogurt

8    2 small plums or 1/2 cup canned fruit in
own juice or water

# WEEK 1: TUESDAY

## 1500 Calories

1   2 slices whole wheat toast
1 tsp. diet jelly
1 cup skim milk

2   1/2 grapefruit

3   2 oz. turkey breast
2 slices whole wheat bread
1 tsp. Miracle Whip (fat free)
1 cup carrot sticks
1 cup celery sticks

4   1 peach or 1/2 cup canned peaches in own juice or water

5   1-1/2 oz. pretzels

6   3. oz. ham
1 baked potato
1 tsp. margarine or 1 tbsp. diet margarine
1/2 cup peas
1/2 cup beets
1 cup skim milk

7   Salad:
1 cup lettuce
1/2 tomato
1/2 cucumber
1/2 cup alfalfa sprouts
1 tbsp. fat-free dressing

8   3 graham crackers (2.5″ square)
1/2 cup fruit juice

# WEEK 1: WEDNESDAY

## 1500 Calories

1. 1 cup Bran Flakes
   1 cup skim milk

2. 1/2 cup orange juice

3. 1/2 cup tuna
   1 pita bread
   1 tsp. Miracle Whip (fat free)
   1 medium tomato

4. 2 tbsp. raisins
   2 tbsp. sunflower seeds

5. 6 vanilla wafers
   1/2 cup skim milk

6. 3 oz. chicken breast
   1 cup (cooked) rice with 1 tsp. margarine
     or 1 tbsp. diet margarine
   1 cup broccoli
   1/2 cup mushrooms
   1/2 cup skim milk

7. 15 grapes

8. 3 cups (air popped) popcorn or microwave
     with less than 2 grams of fat per 3 cups

# WEEK 1: THURSDAY

## 1500 Calories

1   2 slices whole wheat toast
2 tsp. margarine or 1 tbsp. diet margarine
1 tsp. diet jam/jelly
1/2 cup apple juice
1 cup skim milk

2   1/2 grapefruit

3   2 oz. turkey breast
2 slices whole wheat bread
1 cup celery sticks
1 medium cucumber

4   4 bread sticks, crisp

5   1/2 cup fat-free yogurt

6   Grilled cheese: 2 oz. fat-free cheese,
     2 slices whole wheat bread (see recipe)
1 pickle
1/2 cup skim milk

7   Salad:
     1 cup lettuce
     1/4 cup radish
     1/2 cup carrots
     1/2 cup broccoli
     2 tbsp. grated parmesan cheese
6 saltine crackers
1 tbsp. fat-free dressing

8   1/2 cup fruit cocktail in its own juice or
     water

# WEEK 1: FRIDAY

## 1500 Calories

1    1 cup Bran Flakes
      1 cup skim milk

2    1/3 cantaloupe

3    2 oz. ham
      2 slices whole wheat bread
      1/2 cup tomato juice
      1 tsp. margarine or 1 tbsp. diet margarine

4    1 medium apple

5    1/2 cup raw cauliflower
      1/2 cup raw broccoli
      1 roll
      1 tbsp. fat-free dressing

6    3 oz. lean flank steak
      1 cup corn
      1 cup green beans
      1/2 cup skim milk

7    1-1/4 cup watermelon cubes or 1/2 cup
        canned fruit in own juice or water

8    12 vanilla wafers
      1/2 cup skim milk

# WEEK 1:  SATURDAY

## 1500 Calories

1 1 cup egg substitute
2 slices whole wheat toast
1 tsp. margarine
1/2 grapefruit
1/2 cup skim milk

2 1 pear

3 8 oz. fat-free yogurt
3 tbsp. Grapenuts

4 Salad:
  1 cup lettuce
  1/2 cup spinach
  1/2 cup broccoli
1 tbsp. fat-free dressing
4 bread sticks

5 1 orange

6 3 oz. fish
2/3 cup (cooked) rice
1/2 cup peas
1/2 cup skim milk
1 tsp. margarine

7 1 cup carrot sticks

8 1 soft pretzel

## WEEK 2

### Meats

- Ham
- Turkey
- Tuna packed in water
- Ground sirloin hamburger
- Skinless chicken breast
- Shrimp
- Pork tenderloin
- Egg substitute
- Beef sirloin steak

### Fruits

- Orange juice
- Raisins
- Strawberries, fresh or frozen
- Cantaloupe
- Apple
- Plums
- Nectarine
- Pears
- Grapefruit
- Fruit juice
- Grapes
- Orange
- Prunes
- Peaches or canned peaches in own juice or in water
- Banana
- Blueberries, fresh or frozen

### Breads/starches

- Bran Flakes
- Bagels
- Whole wheat bread
- Rice (white or brown)
- Popcorn
- Pita bread
- Saltine crackers
- Hamburger bun
- Potato
- Vanilla wafers
- Graham crackers
- Noodles
- Grapenuts
- Pancake mix (complete pancake mix or frozen pancakes with less than 2 grams of fat)
- Frozen soft pretzel

### Vegetables

- Celery
- Green beans
- Lettuce
- Cauliflower
- Radishes
- Green onion
- Cucumber
- Carrots
- Tomatoes
- Canned tomatoes
- Green pepper

Green onion
Asparagus
Broccoli
Mushrooms
Brussels sprouts
Spinach
Peas
Corn

Dairy
Skim milk
Margarine or diet
margarine
Non-fat yogurt

Fat-free cream cheese
Non-fat frozen yogurt
Low-fat cottage cheese

Miscellaneous/
condiments
Pickles
Miracle Whip (fat free)
or mayonnaise
Fat-free dressing
Sugar-free pudding
Sugar-free gelatin
Light syrup

# WEEK 2: SUNDAY

## 1500 Calories

1    1 cup Bran Flakes
1 cup skim milk
1/2 cup orange juice

2    1 bagel
2 tbsp. raisins
1 tbsp. fat-free cream cheese

3    2 oz. ham slice
1 slice whole wheat bread
1 cup celery sticks

4    1-1/4 cup whole strawberries or 1/2 cup
canned fruit in own juice or water

5    3 oz. turkey breast
2/3 cup (cooked) rice
1/2 cup green beans
1/2 cup skim milk
1 tsp. margarine or 1 tbsp. diet margarine

6    Salad:
1 cup lettuce
1/3 cup radish
1/2 cup cauliflower
1/3 cup green onion
1/2 cup cucumber
1 tbsp. fat-free dressing

7    4 oz. non-fat yogurt

8    3 cups (air popped) popcorn or microwave
less than 2 grams of fat per 3 cups

# WEEK 2: MONDAY

## 1500 Calories

1    1/2 cup Bran Flakes
1/2 cup skim milk
1/3 cup cantaloupe

2    1 apple

3    1 cup carrot sticks

4    1/2 cup tuna
1 pita bread
1 tomato
Lettuce
1 pickle
1 tbsp. Miracle Whip (fat free)

5    1 cup vegetable soup (see recipe)
6 saltine crackers

6    3 oz. lean ground sirloin hamburger
1 hamburger bun
1 serving steak fries (see recipe)
1/2 cup asparagus
1 cup skim milk
1 tsp. margarine or 1 tbsp. diet margarine

7    2 plums or 1/2 cup canned fruit in juice or
water

8    12 vanilla wafers
1/2 cup skim milk

# WEEK 2: TUESDAY

## 1500 Calories

1     2 slices whole wheat toast
       1 cup skim milk
       1/2 cup orange juice

2     1 pear

3     2 oz. turkey
       2 slices whole wheat bread
       1 tomato

4     1 cup raw broccoli
       1 tbsp. fat-free dressing

5     6 graham crackers (2.5" square)

6     3 oz. chicken breast
       1 cup noodles
       1/2 cup sauteed mushrooms
       1/2 cup brussels sprouts
       1 cup skim milk

7     1/2 cup sugar-free vanilla pudding

8     1 nectarine

# WEEK 2: WEDNESDAY

## 1500 Calories

1   1 cup Bran Flakes
1 cup skim milk

2   1/2 grapefruit

3   2 oz. sliced ham
2 slices whole wheat bread
1 cup celery sticks

4   1/2 bagel
1/2 cup fruit juice
2 tsp. fat-free cream cheese

5   Salad:
1 cup spinach
1/3 cup celery
1/3 cup mushrooms
1 tbsp. fat-free dressing

6   3 oz. shrimp
2/3 cup (cooked) rice
1/2 cup cooked carrots
1/2 cup peas
1 cup skim milk
1 tsp. margarine or 1 tbsp. diet margarine

7   15 grapes

8   3 oz. non-fat frozen yogurt

# WEEK 2: THURSDAY

## 1500 Calories

1   1 bagel
    1 tsp. diet jelly
    1 cup skim milk

2   1 orange

3   1 cup raw cauliflower
    1 cup raw broccoli
    1 tbsp. fat-free dressing
    6 saltine crackers

4   1/2 cup tuna
    1 pita bread
    1 tsp. Miracle Whip (fat free)
    Tomato
    Lettuce

5   3 medium prunes or 2 tbsp. raisins

6   3 oz. pork tenderloin
    1/2 cup corn
    1/2 cup noodles, cooked
    1/2 cup green beans
    1 tsp. margarine or 1 tbsp. diet margarine

7   8 oz. non-fat yogurt
    2 tbsp. Grapenuts
    1-1/4 cup whole strawberries (sliced, fresh
      or frozen)

8   1/2 cup sugar-free vanilla pudding

# WEEK 2: FRIDAY

## 1500 Calories

1   1/2 cup egg substitute
    2 slices whole wheat toast
    1 tsp. margarine or 1 tbsp. diet margarine
    1 tsp. diet jelly
    1 cup skim milk

2   1/2 grapefruit

3   1 cup vegetable soup (see recipe)
    12 saltine crackers
    1 cup celery sticks

4   1/2 cup low-fat cottage cheese
    1/2 cup peach slices canned in own juice
       or water
    1 bagel
    1 tsp. fat-free cream cheese

5   1 pear

6   1 medium baked potato
    1 cup broccoli cooked
    2 oz. diet cheese, melted
    1/2 cup skim milk

7   6 graham crackers
    1/2 cup skim milk

8   1 serving sugar-free gelatin

# WEEK 2:  SATURDAY

## 1500 Calories

1    4 pancakes (4" across)
3/4 cup blueberries
1 tbsp. light syrup
1 cup skim milk

2    1 9-inch banana

3    12 vanilla wafers
1/2 cup skim milk

4    1 bagel
2 oz. fat-free cheese

5    Salad:
1 cup lettuce
1 cup spinach
1/3 cup green peppers
2 tbsp. fat-free dressing

6    3 oz. lean beef sirloin
1/2 cup peas
1/2 cup corn
1/2 cup skim milk

7    1 cup raw carrots

8    1 soft pretzel

# WEEK 3

## Meats
Tuna packed in water
Chicken
Turkey
Fish
Ham
Beef sirloin
Pork tenderloin
Shrimp
Healthy Choice hot
dogs

## Fruits
Orange juice
Prunes
Fruit juice
Orange
Apple
Pears
Strawberries, fresh or
frozen
Banana
Grapes
Fruit cocktail packed
in own juice or in
water
Grapefruit
Pineapple chunks
packed in own juice
or in water
Cantaloupe

## Breads/starches
Bran Flakes
Pita bread
Rice (white or brown)
Graham crackers
Whole wheat bread
Popcorn
Bagel
Grapenuts
Bread sticks
Potatoes
Whole wheat crackers
Frozen soft pretzel
Noodles
Vanilla wafers
Pancake mix (complete
pancake mix or
frozen pancakes
with less than 2
grams of fat)
Saltine crackers
Hot dog buns

## Vegetables
Celery
Spinach
Cucumber
Beets
Carrots
Tomatoes
Green beans
Corn
Tomato juice
Green peppers
Cauliflower
Squash

Lettuce
Mushrooms
Broccoli
Brussels sprouts
Green pepper
Green onion
Canned tomatoes
Radishes
Sauerkraut

## Dairy

Skim milk
Non-fat yogurt
Margarine or diet
    margarine

Non-fat frozen yogurt
Low-fat cottage cheese
Fat-free cream cheese
Parmesan cheese

## Miscellaneous/condiments

Miracle Whip (fat free)
    or mayonnaise
Fat-free dressing
Pickle relish
Dijon mustard
Sugar-free pudding
Light syrup

# WEEK 3: SUNDAY

## 1500 Calories

1   1/2 cup egg substitute
    2 slices whole wheat toast
    1 cup skim milk
    1 tsp. margarine or 1 tbsp. diet margarine

2   1/3 cantaloupe

3   6 vanilla wafers
    1/2 cup skim milk

4   2 Healthy Choice hot dogs
    2 hot dog buns
    1/2 cup sauerkraut

5   1 cup carrot sticks

6   3 oz. lean beef sirloin
    1 cup mashed potatoes
    1/2 cup cooked spinach
    1/2 cup sauteed mushrooms

7   1 9-inch banana

8   4 oz. non-fat yogurt

# WEEK 3: MONDAY

## 1500 Calories

1     1 cup Bran Flakes
      1 cup skim milk
      1/2 cup orange juice

2     1-1/2 oz. pretzels
      1/2 cup fruit juice

3     1 cup celery sticks

4     1/2 cup tuna
      1 pita bread
      1 tsp. Miracle Whip (fat free)
      1 pickle

5     Salad:
         1 cup spinach
         1/2 cup cucumber
      1 tbsp. fat-free dressing

6     3 oz. chicken
      2/3 cup rice (cooked)
      1/2 cup beets
      1 cup skim milk
      1 tsp. margarine or 1 tbsp. diet margarine

7     3 prunes or 1/2 cup canned fruit in juice or
        water

8     3 graham crackers (2.5" square)
      1/2 cup skim milk

# WEEK 3: TUESDAY

## 1500 Calories

1    2 slices whole wheat toast
      1 orange
      1 cup skim milk
      1 tsp. margarine or 1 tbsp. diet margarine

2    1 cup carrot sticks

3    1 pear

4    2 oz. turkey breast
      2 slices whole wheat bread
      1 slice tomato
      1 cup raw broccoli
      1 tbsp. fat-free dressing

5    1 bagel
      2 tbsp. fat-free cream cheese
      1 cup skim milk

6    3 oz. fish (baked or grilled)
      1/2 cup green beans
      1/2 cup corn

7    1 baked apple (see recipe)

8    3 cups (air popped) popcorn or microwave
        with 2 grams of fat or less per 3 cups

# WEEK 3: WEDNESDAY

## 1500 Calories

1   1 cup Bran Flakes
     1 cup skim milk
     1/2 cup orange juice

2   4 oz. non-fat yogurt
     3 tbsp. Grapenuts
     1/2 banana (9") or 1 petite banana

3   1/2 cup tomato juice

4   2 oz. ham slice
     2 slices whole wheat bread
     3/4 oz. pretzels

5   2 bread sticks
     1 tsp. margarine
     1/2 cup green peppers (cut in strips)
     1/2 cup raw cauliflower
     1 tbsp. fat-free dressing (for dipping
       vegetables)

6   3 oz. lean beef sirloin
     1 serving steak fries (see recipe)
     1/2 cup green beans
     1/2 cup squash
     1/2 cup skim milk

7   Salad:
       1 cup spinach
       1 cup lettuce
       1/2 cup mushrooms
     1 tbsp. fat-free dressing

8   3 oz. non-fat frozen yogurt
     1-1/4 cup whole strawberries sliced or 1/3
       cup canned pineapple chunks in own
       juice or water

# WEEK 3: THURSDAY

## 1500 Calories

1    2 slices whole wheat toast
     1 cup skim milk
     1 tsp. margarine or 1 tbsp. diet margarine

2    30 grapes

3    1 cup carrot sticks

4    1/2 cup tuna
     2 slices whole wheat bread
     1 tsp. mustard
     1 tsp. pickle relish

5    12 whole wheat crackers
     1 tbsp. salsa

6    3 oz. chicken
     2/3 cup (cooked) rice
     1 cup broccoli
     1 cup skim milk

7    1/2 cup fruit cocktail in own juice or water

8    1 soft pretzel

# WEEK 3: FRIDAY

## 1500 Calories

1   1 cup Bran Flakes
     1 cup skim milk
     1/2 cup orange juice

2   1/2 cup grapefruit or 1/2 cup grapefruit
      juice

3   1 cup celery sticks
     1 cucumber

4   Vegetarian pita (see recipe)

5   1/2 cup low-fat cottage cheese
     1/3 cup pineapple chunks in its own juice
      or water

6   3 oz. pork tenderloin
     1 cup noodles
     1/2 cup brussels sprouts
     1/2 cup skim milk

7   1/2 cup sugar-free pudding
     6 vanilla wafers

8   1 bagel
     1/2 cup skim milk
     1 tbsp. fat-free cream cheese

# WEEK 3: SATURDAY

## 1500 Calories

1   4 pancakes (4" across)
    Light syrup
    1 cup skim milk
    1/2 cup orange juice

2   1 pear

3   1 cup vegetable soup (see recipe)
    12 saltine crackers

4   2 oz. chicken
    2/3 cup (cooked) rice
    1/2 cup cooked celery

5   15 grapes

6   2 oz. shrimp
    1 cup fettucine noodles (cooked)
    1/3 cup parmesan cheese
    1/2 cup skim milk
    1 tsp. margarine or 1 tbsp. diet margarine

7   Salad:
        1 cup lettuce
        1/2 cup cucumber
        1/4 cup radish
    1 tbsp. fat-free dressing

8   3 graham crackers (2.5" squares)
    1/2 cup skim milk

# WEEK 4

## Meats

Turkey
Chicken
Egg substitute
Tuna packed in water
Fish
Ham
Healthy Choice hot
dogs
Flank steak

## Fruits

Orange juice
Pineapple chunks
packed in own juice
or in water
Cantaloupe
Grapefruit or grapefruit
juice
Grapes
Apples
Bananas
Prunes
Pears
Raisins
Orange
Plums
Fruit juice
Strawberries (fresh or
frozen)

## Breads/starches

Whole wheat bread
Potatoes
Bagel
Bread sticks
English muffins

Flour tortilla shells (7
inches)
Pita bread
Saltine crackers
Popcorn
Rice (white or brown)
Bran Flakes
Vanilla wafers
Hot dog buns
Noodles
Grapenuts
Pancake mix (complete
pancake mix or
frozen pancakes
with less than 2
grams of fat)
Frozen soft pretzel

## Vegetables

Celery
Tomato juice
Broccoli
Lettuce
Green onions
Zucchini
Bean sprouts
Tomatoes
Canned tomatoes
Green peppers
Cucumber

Carrots
Corn
Mushrooms
Spinach
Alfalfa sprouts
Green beans
Sauerkraut
Tomato juice
Asparagus

## Dairy

Margarine or diet
   margarine
Skim milk
Fat-free shredded
   cheddar cheese
Fat-free cream cheese
Low-fat cottage cheese

Fat-free yogurt
Non-fat frozen yogurt

## Miscellaneous/ condiments

Diet jelly or jam
Fat-free pudding
Lemon juice
Weight Watchers Smart
   One Lemon Herb
   Chicken
Salsa
Honey
Miracle Whip (fat free)
   or mayonnaise
Fat-free dressing
Fig Newtons
Light syrup

# WEEK 4: SUNDAY

## 1500 Calories

1  2 slices whole wheat toast
   1 tsp. diet jelly or 1 tbsp. diet margarine
   1 cup skim milk
   1 tsp. margarine

2  1/2 cup orange juice

3  3 oz. sliced turkey
   2 slices whole wheat bread
   1 cup celery sticks

4  2/3 cup pineapple chunks in own juice or
      water

5  1 cup tomato juice

6  1 large baked potato
   2 oz. fat-free shredded cheddar cheese,
      melted over broccoli and potato
   1/2 cup broccoli

7  1 bagel
   1 cup skim milk
   2 tbsp. fat-free cream cheese

8  1/2 cup fat-free pudding

# WEEK 4: MONDAY

## 1500 Calories

1. 2 slices whole wheat toast
   1/3 cantaloupe
   2 tsp. diet jam or jelly
   1 cup skim milk

2. 1-1/2 oz. pretzels

3. Salad:
   1 cup lettuce
   1/4 cup green onions
   1/4 cup zucchini
   4 bread sticks
   1 tsp. margarine or 1 tbsp. diet margarine
   2 tbsp. lemon juice

4. 1/2 grapefruit or 1/2 cup grapefruit juice

5. Weight Watchers Smart One Lemon Herb Chicken
   1 cup skim milk

6. 1/2 cup low-fat cottage cheese

7. 16 tortilla chips (see recipe)
   4 tablespoons salsa

8. 15 grapes

# WEEK 4: TUESDAY

## 1500 Calories

1    1 English muffin
1/2 cup egg substitute
1 tsp. honey
1/2 cup skim milk

2    4 oz. non-fat yogurt

3    3 oz. chicken
1 pita bread
1/2 cup bean sprouts
Lettuce
5 olives
2 slices tomato

4    Baked apple (see recipe)

5    1 bagel
1 cup skim milk
1 tbsp. fat-free cream cheese

6    1 cup vegetable soup (see recipe)
9 saltine crackers
1 oz. fat-free cheese

7    1 9" banana

8    3 cups (air popped) popcorn or microwave popcorn with 2 grams of fat or less per 3 cups

# WEEK 4: WEDNESDAY

## 1500 Calories

1    2 slices whole wheat toast
1/3 cantaloupe
1 cup skim milk
1 tsp. margarine or 1 tbsp. diet margarine

2    1/2 cup carrot sticks
1/2 cup celery sticks

3    1/2 cup tuna
1 bagel
1 tsp. Miracle Whip (fat free)

4    3 prunes or 2 tbsp. raisins

5    3 oz. fish (baked or grilled)
2/3 cup (cooked) rice
1/2 cup corn

6    Salad:
        1 cup lettuce
        1 cup spinach
        1/2 cup mushrooms
        1/2 cup alfalfa sprouts
        1/2 cup cucumber
    2 tbsp. fat-free dressing

7    2 Fig Newtons
1 cup skim milk

8    1 pear

# WEEK 4: THURSDAY

## 1500 Calories

1    1 cup Bran Flakes
2 tbsp. raisins
1 cup skim milk

2    1 orange

3    2 oz. ham
2 slices whole wheat bread
1 tomato
Lettuce

4    1 cup vegetable soup (see recipe)
2 bread sticks (crisp)

5    6 vanilla wafers
1 cup skim milk

6    3 oz. turkey breast
1/2 cup green beans
1 cup mashed potatoes
1 tsp. margarine or 1 tbsp. diet margarine

7    1 apple

8    1/2 cup non-fat frozen yogurt

# WEEK 4: FRIDAY

## 1500 Calories

1   2 slices whole wheat toast
    1 cup skim milk
    2 tsp. margarine or 1 tbsp. diet margarine

2   1 grapefruit or 1 cup grapefruit juice

3   2 Healthy Choice hot dogs
    2 hot dog buns
    1/2 cup sauerkraut

4   2 plums or 2 tbsp. raisins

5   1/2 cup tomato juice

6   3 oz. flank steak
    1 cup noodles, cooked
    1/2 cup broccoli
    1/2 cup skim milk

7   1/2 banana (9")

8   4 oz. fat-free yogurt
    3 tbsp. Grapenuts

# WEEK 4: SATURDAY

## 1500 Calories

1    4 pancakes (4" across)
1 tbsp. light syrup
1 cup skim milk

2    6 vanilla wafers
1/2 cup skim milk

3    1/2 cup cottage cheese
1-1/4 cup whole strawberries
6 saltine crackers

4    Salad:
        1 cup lettuce
        1/4 cup celery
        1/4 cup green onions
        1/2 cup cauliflower
        1/2 cup broccoli
2 tbsp. fat-free dressing

5    1 bagel
1/2 cup fruit juice

6    3 oz. chicken breast
2/3 cup (cooked) rice
1/2 cup asparagus
1/2 cup skim milk
1 tsp. margarine or 1 tbsp. diet margarine

7    1/3 cup cantaloupe

8    1 soft pretzel

# VIII

## 1800 CALORIES
### SHOPPING LIST AND MENUS

WEEK 1

Meats
- Turkey breast
- Shrimp
- Pork tenderloin
- Egg substitute
- Tuna packed in water
- Ham
- Ground round hamburger
- Chicken
- Healthy Choice hot dogs
- Fish
- Beef tenderloin

Fruits
- Oranges
- Pears
- Raisins
- Grapefruit or grapefruit juice
- Apple
- Banana
- Pineapple juice
- Fruit cocktail packed in own juice or in water
- Peach or canned peaches packed in own juice or in water
- Cantaloupe
- Blueberries (fresh or frozen)
- Strawberries (fresh or frozen)

Breads
- Whole wheat bread
- Oatmeal
- Rice (white or brown)

Pretzels
Bagels
Wheat grain English
  muffins
Graham crackers
Potatoes
Grapenuts
Bran Flakes
Pita bread
Dinner roll
Saltine crackers
Hamburger bun
Stuffing
Pancake mix (complete
  pancake mix or
  frozen pancakes
  with less than 2
  grams of fat)
Hot dog buns
Noodles
Fig Newtons
Wheat crackers
Bread sticks (crisp)

## Vegetables

Carrots
Lettuce
Mushrooms
Onion
Green pepper
Spinach
Peapods
Cauliflower
Tomato juice

Celery
Tomato
Bean sprouts
Broccoli
Alfalfa sprouts
Cucumbers
Beets
Sauerkraut
Peas
Radish
Green beans

## Dairy

Margarine
Skim milk
Fat-free cream cheese
Low-fat cheese
Non-fat yogurt
Low-fat cottage cheese
Low-fat frozen yogurt

## Miscellaneous/ condiments

Fat-free dressing
Almonds
Peanuts
Pickles
Miracle Whip (fat free)
Weight Watchers
  Lemon Herb
    Chicken Riccata
Sugar-free gelatin
Diet syrup
Natural peanut butter

# WEEK 1: SUNDAY

## 1800 Calories

1    1 cup oatmeal
2 slices whole wheat toast
1 cup skim milk
1 tsp. margarine

2    1 orange

3    1 oz. turkey breast
2 slices whole wheat bread
1 cup carrot sticks

4    1 pear

5    Salad:
1 cup lettuce
1/2 cup mushrooms
1/4 cup onions
1/4 cup green peppers
1 cup spinach
1 tbsp. fat-free dressing

6    4 oz. shrimp
1 cup peapods
2/3 cup (cooked) rice
1 tsp. margarine

7    Snack mix:
6 whole almonds
20 small peanuts
3/4 oz. pretzels
4 tbsp. raisins

8    1 bagel
1 tsp. fat-free cream cheese
1 cup skim milk

# WEEK 1: MONDAY

## 1800 Calories

1   1 wheat grain English muffin
    1 cup skim milk
    1 tsp. margarine

2   1/2 grapefruit or 1/2 cup grapefruit juice

3   2 oz. low-fat cheese
    1 bagel
    1 cup raw cauliflower
    1 tbsp. fat-free dressing

4   1 apple
    6 graham crackers (2.5″ square)
    1/2 cup skim milk

5   1/2 cup tomato juice

6   4 oz. pork tenderloin
    1 large baked potato
    1 cup spinach
    1 tsp. margarine

7   4 oz. non-fat yogurt
    3 tbsp. Grapenuts
    12 wheat crackers

8   1 banana (9 inch)

# WEEK 1: TUESDAY

## 1800 Calories

1   1 cup Bran Flakes
    1 cup skim milk
    1/2 cup egg substitute

2   2/3 cup pineapple chunks in own juice or
    water

3   1/2 cup tuna
    1 pita bread
    1 pickle
    Lettuce
    1 tbsp. Miracle Whip (fat free)
    1 low-fat granola bar

4   1 cup carrot sticks
    1 cup celery sticks
    1 tbsp. fat-free dressing

5   1/2 cup fruit cocktail in own juice and
    water

6   Weight Watchers Lemon Herb Chicken
    Ricotta
    1 dinner roll
    1 cup skim milk

7   1 orange

8   3 cups (air popped) popcorn or microwave
    with less than 2 grams of fat per 3 cups

## WEEK 1: WEDNESDAY

## 1800 Calories

1.  2 slices whole wheat toast
    1 cup skim milk
    1 tsp. margarine

2.  1/2 cup grapefruit or 1/2 cup grapefruit juice

3.  1/2 cup low-fat cottage cheese
    1-1/4 cup whole strawberries
    12 saltine crackers

4.  2 slices whole wheat bread
    2 oz. sliced ham
    1 cup celery sticks

5.  Salad:
    1 cup lettuce
    1/2 tomato
    1/4 cup celery
    1/4 cup bean sprouts
    1 tbsp. fat-free dressing
    2 crisp bread sticks

6.  4 oz. ground round hamburger
    1 hamburger bun
    1/2 cup broccoli
    1/2 cup corn
    1 pickle
    1 cup skim milk
    1 tsp. margarine

7.  30 grapes

8.  1/2 cup low-fat frozen yogurt

# WEEK 1: THURSDAY

## 1800 Calories

1  1/2 cup egg substitute
   1 whole wheat English muffin
   1 cup skim milk
   1 tbsp. diet jelly

2  1 orange

3  2 oz. cubed chicken
   1 pita
   1/2 cup shredded lettuce
   1 cucumber
   1/4 cup alfalfa sprouts
   1 tbsp. fat-free dressing

4  1 pear

5  6 graham crackers (2.5" square)
   1 cup skim milk

6  3 oz. lean turkey
   3/4 cup stuffing
   1 large baked potato
   1/2 cup beets
   1 tsp. margarine

7  3/4 oz. pretzels
   1 cup fruit juice

8  1/2 cup sugar-free gelatin

# WEEK 1: FRIDAY

## 1800 Calories

1. 4 pancakes (4″ across)
   1/2 cup blueberries
   1/2 cup orange juice
   1 cup skim milk
   Diet syrup

2. 1/2 cup celery sticks
   1/2 cup carrot sticks
   1 tbsp. fat-free dressing

3. 2 Healthy Choice hot dogs
   2 hot dog buns
   1/2 cup sauerkraut

4. 1 peach or 1/2 cup canned peaches in own juice or water

5. Salad:
   1 cup lettuce
   1 cup spinach
   1/2 cup mushrooms
   1/2 cup broccoli, 1/2 cup cauliflower
   1 tbsp. fat-free dressing

6. 4 oz. fish
   2/3 cup rice, cooked
   1/2 cup peas
   1 cup skim milk
   1 tsp. margarine

7. 1 baked apple (see recipe)

8. 3 cups (air popped) popcorn or microwave with less than 2 grams of fat per 3 cups

# WEEK 1: SATURDAY

## 1800 Calories

1   1 slices whole wheat toast
    1 cup orange juice
    1 cup Bran Flakes
    1 cup skim milk
    1 tsp. margarine

2   1/3 cantaloupe

3   2 oz. sliced ham
    2 slices whole wheat toast
    Salad
        1 cup lettuce
        1 radish
        1 cucumber
    1 tbsp. fat-free dressing

4   6 saltine crackers
    1 tbsp. natural peanut butter

5   1/2 cup tomato juice

6   3 oz. beef tenderloin
    1 cup noodles, cooked
    1/2 cup green beans
    1 tsp. margarine

7   2 Fig Newtons
    1/2 cup skim milk

8   4 oz. non-fat plain yogurt
    1/3 cup pineapple chunks in juice or water
    2/3 cup strawberries

# WEEK 2

## Meats
- Turkey
- Chicken
- Ham
- Tuna packed in water
- Fish
- Healthy Choice hot dogs

## Fruits
- Raisins
- Apricots
- Oranges
- Apples
- Cantaloupe
- Peach or canned peaches in own juice or in water
- Fruit juice
- Orange juice
- Grapes
- Pear
- Pineapple chunks canned in own juice or in water
- Bananas
- Plums
- Fruit juice
- Grapefruit or grapefruit juice
- Strawberries (fresh or frozen)
- Applesauce

## Breads/starches
- Whole wheat bread
- Bran Flakes
- Noodles
- Grapenuts

- Oatmeal
- Bread sticks (crisp)
- Bagels
- Dinner rolls
- Popcorn
- English muffins
- Pretzels
- Graham crackers
- Low-fat granola bar
- Vanilla wafers
- Saltine crackers
- Fig Newtons
- Potatoes
- Flour tortilla shells (7 inches)
- Pancakes (complete pancake mix or frozen pancakes with less than 2 grams of fat)
- Hot dog buns
- Rice (white or brown)
- Frozen soft pretzel

## Vegetables
- Celery
- Tomatoes
- Lettuce

Broccoli
Corn
Carrots
Cauliflower
Water chestnuts
Zucchini
Spinach
Green peppers
Cucumber
Mushrooms
Beets
Green beans
Brussels sprouts
Red cabbage
Radishes
Asparagus

Dairy
Skim milk
Fat-free yogurt

Fat-free cheese
Margarine
Low-fat cottage cheese
Low-fat frozen yogurt

Miscellaneous/
condiments
Diet jam or jelly
Miracle Whip (fat free)
Sugar-free pudding
Fat-free dressing
Budget Light Oriental
Beef frozen entree
Bean soup
Salsa
Budget Gourmet Light
Sirloin of Beef in
Herb Sauce

# WEEK 2: SUNDAY

## 1800 Calories

1     2 slices whole wheat toast
1 cup Bran Flakes
2 tbsp. raisins
1 cup skim milk
Jam or jelly

2     4 apricots or 1/2 cup canned apricots or 7
      halves dried apricots

3     2 oz. turkey
2 slices whole wheat toast
1 tomato slice
Lettuce
1 orange
1 tbsp. Miracle Whip (fat free)

4     1 cup celery sticks

5     1 apple

6     4 oz. chicken without skin
2/3 cup rice, cooked
1 cup broccoli
1/2 cup corn
1 tsp. margarine

7     8 oz. fat-free yogurt
3 tbsp. Grapenuts

8     1/2 cup sugar-free pudding

# WEEK 2: MONDAY

## 1800 Calories

1    2 slices whole wheat toast
     1/2 cup oatmeal
     1/3 cantaloupe
     1 cup skim milk
     1 tsp. margarine

2    4 bread sticks (crisp)
     1 cup carrot sticks
     1 cup cauliflower
     1 tbsp. fat-free dressing

3    2 oz. ham
     1 bagel
     1 oz. fat-free cheese

4    1 peach or 1/2 cup canned peaches in own
        juice or water

5    Salad:
        1 cup lettuce
        1/2 cup water chestnuts
        1/2 cup zucchini
     1 tbsp. fat-free dressing

6    Budget Light Oriental Beef
     1 dinner roll
     1 cup skim milk
     1 tsp. margarine

7    1 cup fruit cocktail in own juice or water

8    3 cups (air popped) popcorn or microwave
        with less than 2 grams of fat per 3 cups

# WEEK 2: TUESDAY

## 1800 Calories

1   1 English muffin
    1 cup skim milk
    1/2 cup orange juice
    1 tsp. margarine

2   15 grapes

3   3 oz. turkey
    2 slices whole wheat bread
    1/2 cup fat-free yogurt
    1-1/2 oz. pretzels

4   2 graham crackers (2.5" square)
    1/2 cup skim milk

5   Salad:
        1 cup spinach
        1/4 cup green peppers
        1/2 cup cucumber
        1/2 cup mushrooms
        1/2 cup beets
    1 tbsp. fat-free dressing

6   2 slices whole wheat bread
    2 oz. fat-free cheese
    1/2 cup green beans
    1/2 cup bean soup
    1 tsp. margarine

7   1 pear

8   1/4 cup low-fat cottage cheese
    1/3 cup pineapple chunks in juice or water

# WEEK 2: WEDNESDAY

## 1800 Calories

1    1 cup Bran Flakes
1/2 banana (9")
1 cup skim milk
1 orange

2    1 low-fat granola bar

3    1/2 cup tuna
1 bagel
1 slice tomato
Lettuce
1 cup carrot sticks
1 cucumber
1 tbsp. Miracle Whip (fat free)

4    2 plums or 1/2 cup canned fruit in own
juice or water

5    12 vanilla wafers
1/2 cup skim milk

6    4 oz. ham
1 cup mashed potatoes
1/2 cup brussels sprouts
1//2 cup skim milk
2 tsp. margarine

7    6 saltine crackers
1/2 cup fruit juice

8    1/2 cup low-fat frozen yogurt

# WEEK 2: THURSDAY

## 1800 Calories

1    2 slices whole wheat toast
1 cup skim milk
1 tsp. diet jelly or jam
1 tsp. margarine

2    1 grapefruit or 1 cup grapefruit juice

3    3 oz. chicken
2 slices whole wheat bread
1 Fig Newton
1 tbsp. Miracle Whip (fat free)

4    1 apple

5    Salad:
    1 cup lettuce
    1/2 cup carrots
    1/2 cup red cabbage
    1/4 cup raisins
1 tbsp. fat-free dressing
4 bread sticks (crisp)

6    1 large baked potato
3 oz. fat-free cheese, melted
1 cup broccoli
1 tsp. margarine

7    8 oz . fat-free yogurt
1-1/4 cup whole strawberries (fresh or
    frozen)

8    16 tortilla chips (see recipe)
2 tbsp. salsa

# WEEK 2: FRIDAY

## 1800 Calories

1   Omelet:
    1/2 cup egg substitute
    1/2 cup diced tomatoes
    1/4 cup mushrooms
    1/4 cup diced green peppers
    1/4 cup celery
    2 slices whole wheat toast
    1 cup skim milk
    1 tsp. margarine

2   1/2 cup fat-free yogurt
    3 tbsp. Grapenuts

3   1/2 cup low-fat cottage cheese
    1/2 cup pineapple chunks in juice or water

4   Vegetable mix:
    2/3 cup rice, cooked
    1/2 cup corn
    1/4 cup green pepper
    1/2 cup French cut green beans

5   12 saltine crackers
    1 oz. fat-free cheese
    15 grapes

6   Budget Gourmet Light Sirloin of Beef in
    Herb Sauce
    1 diced tomato
    1 dinner roll
    1 tsp. margarine

7   4 apricots or 1/2 cup canned apricots or 7
    halves dried apricots

8   3 graham crackers (2.5" square)
    1/2 cup skim milk

# WEEK 2: SATURDAY

## 1800 Calories

1. 4 pancakes (4" across)
   1 cup skim milk
   1 tsp. margarine
   Diet syrup

2. 1 orange

3. 2 Healthy Choice hot dogs
   2 hot dog buns
   1/2 cup baked beans
   1/2 cup cooked spinach

4. 1 cup lettuce
   1 cup cauliflower
   2 bread sticks (crisp)
   1 tbsp. fat-free dressing

5. 1 banana (9")

6. 4 oz. fish
   2/3 cup rice, cooked
   1 cup asparagus
   1 cup skim milk
   1 tsp. margarine

7. 1/2 cup applesauce

8. 1 soft pretzel

# WEEK 3

## Meats
Tuna packed in water
Turkey
Shrimp
Ham
Ground round
Chicken
Pork tenderloin
Eggs
Fish

## Fruits
Raisins
Fruit juice
Peaches or canned peaches in own juice or in water
Raspberries (If not in season may substitute 1/2 c. canned fruit in own juice or in water)
Apple juice
Plums
Orange
Fruit cocktail packed in own juice or in water
Orange juice
Grapes
Pear
Blueberries (fresh or frozen)
Watermelon (If not in season may substitute with 1/2 c. canned fruit in own juice or in water)
Cantaloupe
Applesauce
Prunes
Strawberries (fresh or frozen)
Pineapple chunks packed in own juice or in water
Orange juice
Banana

## Breads
Bran Flakes
Whole wheat bread
Pita bread
Stuffing
Popcorn
Noodles
Oatmeal
Vanilla wafers
Whole wheat English muffins
Pretzels
Corn muffin
Tortilla Shells
Low-fat crackers
Rice (white or brown)
Dinner roll
Pancakes (complete

pancake mix or
frozen pancakes
with less than 2
grams of fat)
Muffin
Grapenuts
Garlic bread
Flour tortilla shells (7
inches)
Bread sticks (crisp)

## Vegetables

Lettuce
Carrot
Celery
Squash
Brussels sprouts
Broccoli
Mixed vegetables
Cucumbers
Tomatoes
Green onion
Alfalfa sprouts
Spinach
Tomato juice
Peas
Radish

Mushrooms
Cauliflower

## Dairy

Skim milk
Non-fat yogurt
Fat-free frozen yogurt
Fat-free cream cheese
Margarine
Low-fat cottage cheese
Fat-free cheese

## Miscellaneous/ condiments

Miracle Whip (fat free)
Fat-free refried beans
Salsa
Sugar-free gelatin
Diet jam or jelly
Fat-free dressing
Peanut butter
Stouffer's Lean Cuisine
   Breast of Chicken
   Parmesan
Sugar-free pudding
Diet syrup

# WEEK 3: SUNDAY

## 1800 Calories

1   1 cup Bran Flakes
    1 slice whole wheat toast
    1 tbsp. raisins
    1 cup skim milk

2   1/3 cantaloupe

3   1/2 cup tuna
    1 pita bread
    Lettuce
    1/2 cup fruit juice
    1 tbsp. Miracle Whip (fat free)

4   1 cup carrot sticks
    1 cup celery sticks

5   1 peach or 1/2 cup canned peaches in juice
        or water

6   4 oz. turkey
    3/4 cup stuffing
    1/2 cup squash
    1/2 cup brussels sprouts
    1 dinner roll
    1/2 cup skim milk

7   4 oz. non-fat yogurt
    1 cup raspberries or 1/2 cup canned fruit
        in juice or water
    3 tbsp. Grapenuts

8   3 cups (air popped) popcorn or microwave
        with 2 grams or less of fat per 3 cups

# WEEK 3: MONDAY

## 1800 Calories

1    2 slices whole wheat toast
1/2 cup oatmeal
1/2 cup apple juice
1/2 cup skim milk
1 tsp. margarine

2    2 plums

3    2 oz. sliced ham
2 slices whole wheat bread
1 cup raw broccoli
1 tbsp. fat-free dressing

4    1 bagel
1 tbsp. fat-free cream cheese
1/2 cup skim milk

5    1 orange

6    4 oz. shrimp
1 cup noodles
1 cup mixed vegetables
1 tsp. margarine

7    1/2 cup fruit cocktail in juice or water

8    12 vanilla wafers
1 cup skim milk

# WEEK 3: TUESDAY

## 1800 Calories

1    1 whole grain English muffin
1 cup skim milk
1/2 cup orange juice
1 tsp. margarine

2    15 grapes

3    2 oz. turkey
2 slices whole wheat bread
1 cucumber
1 cup skim milk

4    1-1/2 oz. pretzels

5    1 pear

6    3 oz. ground round hamburger
1/2 cup fat-free refried beans
1 corn muffin
2 tortilla shells
2 tbsp. salsa
1 cup shredded lettuce
1 diced tomato
1 oz. fat-free cheese
1/4 cup green onion

7    1/2 cup fat-free frozen yogurt
3/4 cup blueberries

8    1/2 cup sugar-free gelatin

## WEEK 3: WEDNESDAY

### 1800 Calories

1  2 slices whole wheat toast
   1 cup skim milk
   1 tsp. diet jam or jelly
   1 tsp. margarine

2  1-1/4 cup watermelon cubes or 1/2 cup
   canned fruit in juice or water

3  2 oz. chicken diced
   1 pita
   1/2 cup tomato slices
   1/4 cup alfalfa sprouts
   1/2 cup cucumber
   1/2 cup lettuce
   1 tbsp. fat-free dressing

4  1/2 cup low-fat cottage cheese
   1/3 cantaloupe
   12 low-fat crackers

5  6 graham crackers (2.5″ square)
   1/2 cup fruit juice

6  4 oz. pork tenderloin
   2/3 cup rice
   1/2 cup spinach
   1 slice bread
   1/2 cup skim milk
   1 tsp. margarine

7  1/2 cup applesauce

8  4 oz. fat-free yogurt

# WEEK 3: THURSDAY

## 1800 Calories

1  1 cup Bran Flakes
   1 cup skim milk
   1 slice whole wheat toast
   1 soft-boiled egg
   1/2 cup orange juice
   1 tsp. margarine

2  1 peach or 1/2 cup canned peaches in own
   juice or in water

3  1 bagel
   2 oz. fat-free cheese
   1 cup celery sticks
   1 tbsp. peanut butter

4  6 vanilla wafers
   1/2 cup skim milk

5  3/4 oz. pretzels
   1/2 cup fruit juice

6  Stouffer's Lean Cuisine Breast of Chicken
   Parmesan
   1 dinner roll
   1/2 cup skim milk

7  2 medium prunes or 3 tbsp. raisins or 2
   plums

8  1/2 cup sugar-free pudding

# WEEK 3: FRIDAY

## 1800 Calories

1    4 pancakes (4" across)
1-1/4 cup whole strawberries (sliced, fresh or frozen)
1 cup skim milk
Diet syrup

2    1/2 cup tomato juice

3    1 muffin

4    Salad:
     1 cup lettuce
     1 cup spinach
     1/2 cup tuna
     1/2 cup cucumber slices
     1/4 cup radish
   6 bread sticks (crisp)
   1 tbsp. fat-free dressing

5    15 grapes

6    4 oz. fish
2/3 cup rice
1/2 cup carrots
1/2 cup peas
1 cup skim milk
1 tsp. margarine

7    1/3 cantaloupe

8    1/2 cup fat-free frozen yogurt
1/3 cup pineapple chunks in own juice or water
3 tbsp. Grapenuts

# WEEK 3: SATURDAY

## 1800 Calories

1   1 egg omelet with 1 oz. fat-free cheese
    1 whole grain English muffin
    1/2 cup orange juice
    1 tsp. margarine

2   6 graham crackers (2.5″ square)
    1 cup skim milk

3   1/4 cup low-fat cottage cheese
    1/2 cup canned peach slices in juice or
        water

4   1 bagel
    1 tbsp. fat-free cream cheese
    1 cup carrot sticks
    1/2 cup skim milk

5   Salad:
        1 cup spinach
        1/2 cup mushroom
        1/4 cup celery
        1/2 cup cauliflower
    1 tbsp. fat-free dressing

6   3 oz. ground round hamburger
    1/2 cup spaghetti sauce
    1 cup noodles
    1 slice garlic bread
    1/2 cup skim milk
    1 tsp. margarine

7   1 banana (9″)

8   16 tortilla chips (see recipe)
    2 tbsp. salsa

## WEEK 4

Meats
- Ham
- Turkey
- Chicken
- Pork tenderloin
- Tuna packed in water
- Fish
- Eggs
- Beef tenderloin
- Healthy Choice hot dog
- Cornish hen

Fruits
- Orange
- Pineapple chunks packed in own juice or in water
- Pears
- Fruit juice
- Peaches or canned peaches in own juice or in water
- Orange juice
- Apples
- Raisins
- Grapes
- Plums
- Fruit cocktail packed in own juice or in water
- Applesauce
- Grapefruit or grapefruit juice
- Banana
- Blueberries (fresh or frozen)
- Prunes

Breads
- Bran Flakes
- Whole wheat bread
- Pretzels
- Bread sticks (crisp)
- Dinner roll
- Popcorn
- Bagel
- Graham crackers
- Saltine crackers
- Garlic bread
- Pita bread
- Potatoes
- Noodles
- English muffin
- Muffin
- Vanilla wafers
- Rice (white or brown)
- Low-fat crackers
- Pancakes (complete pancake mix or frozen pancakes with less than 2 grams of fat)
- Grapenuts
- Hot dog buns

Vegetables
- Lettuce
- Tomatoes
- Tomato juice
- Corn
- Broccoli
- Cucumbers
- Green pepper
- Green onion
- Canned tomatoes
- Beets
- Peas
- Carrots
- Celery
- Mushrooms
- Radish
- Cauliflower
- Sauerkraut
- Green beans

Dairy
- Low-fat cheese
- Skim milk

Margarine
Non-fat frozen yogurt
Fat-free cream cheese
Egg
Fat-free yogurt
Low-fat cottage cheese

Miscellaneous/
condiments
- Diet jam or jelly
- Weight Watchers Smart One Lasagna Florentine
- Sugar-free gelatin
- Dijon mustard
- Low-fat granola bars
- Fig Newtons
- Miracle Whip (fat free)
- Fat-free salad dressing
- Peanut butter
- Sugar-free pudding

# WEEK 4: SUNDAY

## 1800 Calories

1    1 cup Bran Flakes
1 slice whole wheat toast
1 cup skim milk
1 tsp. diet jam or jelly

2    1 orange

3    3 oz. sliced ham
2 slices whole wheat bread
1 slice tomato
Lettuce
3/4 oz. pretzels
1/2 cup skim milk
1 cucumber

4    2/3 cup pineapple chunks in juice or water

5    1/2 cup tomato juice
2 bread sticks (crisp)

6    3 oz. turkey
1 cup corn
1/2 cup broccoli
1/2 cup skim milk
1 dinner roll

7    1 pear

8    3 cups (air popped) popcorn or microwave
with 2 grams of fat or less per 3 cups

# WEEK 4: MONDAY

## 1800 Calories

1.     2 slices whole wheat toast
    1/2 cup fruit juice
    1 cup skim milk
    1 tsp. margarine
    Jam or jelly

2.     1/2 grapefruit or 1/2 cup grapefruit juice

3.     1/2 cup low-fat cottage cheese
    1 oz. chicken
    1 bagel
    1/2 cup canned peaches in own juice or
       water or 1 peach

4.     6 graham crackers (2.5" square)
    1/2 cup skim milk

5.     1 cup vegetable soup (see recipe)
    12 saltine crackers

6.     Weight Watchers Smart One Lasagna
       Florentine
    1 slice garlic bread
    1/2 cup skim milk

7.     3 prunes or 1/2 cup canned fruit in juice or
       water

8.     1/2 cup sugar-free gelatin

# WEEK 4: TUESDAY

## 1800 Calories

1   1 cup Bran Flakes
    2 tbsp. raisins
    1/2 cup skim milk

2   1/2 cup orange juice

3   Vegetable pita
        1 cup lettuce
        1/2 cup beets
        1/2 cup cucumber slices
        1/2 tomato sliced
        1 tbsp. fat-free mayonnaise
        1 tsp. dijon mustard
    15 grapes

4   1 low-fat granola bar
    1/2 cup skim milk

5   1 large baked potato
    2 oz. melted low-fat cheese
    1/2 cup broccoli
    1/2 cup skim milk

6   4 oz. pork tenderloin
    1 cup noodles
    1/2 cup peas
    1/2 cup carrots
    1 tsp. margarine

7   1 apple

8   3/4 oz. pretzels

# WEEK 4: WEDNESDAY

## 1800 Calories

1    1 English muffin
2 plums
1 cup skim milk
1 tsp. margarine

2    1 muffin

3    1/2 cup tuna
1 cup carrot sticks
1 bagel
6 vanilla wafers
Lettuce
1 tsp. Miracle Whip (fat free)

4    1/2 cup fruit cocktail

5    1 cup celery sticks
1 cup broccoli florets
1 tbsp. fat-free dressing

6    4 oz. chicken
2/3 cup rice
1/2 cup corn
1 cup skim milk
1 tsp. margarine

7    1/2 cup applesauce

8    12 low-fat crackers
1/2 cup fruit juice

# WEEK 4: THURSDAY

## 1800 Calories

1   1 cup Bran Flakes
1 cup skim milk
1/2 cup orange juice

2   1 pear

3   3 oz. sliced turkey
2 slices whole wheat bread
1 tbsp. Miracle Whip (fat free)

4   2 Fig Newtons
1/2 cup skim milk

5   Salad:
     1 cup spinach
     1/4 cup mushrooms
     1/4 cup radish
     1/2 cup cauliflower
2 bread sticks (crisp)
1 tbsp. fat-free dressing

6   3 oz. fish
1 large baked potato
1/2 cub beets
1 slice whole wheat bread
1/2 cup skim milk
2 tsp. margarine

7   30 grapes

8   1/2 cup non-fat frozen yogurt

## WEEK 4: FRIDAY

## 1800 Calories

1   1 egg
    2 slices whole wheat toast
    1 tbsp. peanut butter
    1 cup skim milk
    1/2 cup fruit juice

2   1/2 grapefruit or 1/2 cup grapefruit juice

3   Salad:
        1 cup lettuce
        1/4 cup celery
        1/4 cup onion
        1 tomato
    1 tbsp. fat-free dressing
    6 saltine crackers

4   1 bagel
    1 tbsp. fat-free cream cheese
    1/2 cup skim milk

5   1 cup vegetable soup (see recipe)
    2 bread sticks (crisp)
    1/2 cup skim milk

6   4 oz. beef tenderloin
    1/2 cup brussels sprouts
    1 cup noodles
    1/2 cup peas

7   1 banana (9″)

8   1/2 cup sugar-free pudding
    6 vanilla wafers

# WEEK 4: SATURDAY

## 1800 Calories

1   4 pancakes (4″ across)
    3/4 blueberries (fresh or frozen)
    1 cup skim milk
    Diet syrup

2   1/2 cup orange juice

3   2 Healthy Choice hot dogs
    2 hot dog buns
    1/2 cup sauerkraut
    1 apple

4   1 cup carrot sticks
    1 cup broccoli
    1 tbsp. fat-free dressing

5   1/2 cup fruit juice
    6 low-fat crackers

6   4 oz. Cornish hen (without skin)
    2/3 cup rice
    1/2 cup green beans
    1/2 cup skim milk
    1 tsp. margarine

7   1/2 cup fat-free yogurt
    2 tbsp. Grapenuts

8   3 cups (air popped) popcorn or
        microwave with 2 grams of fat or less
        per 3 cups

# IX

# RECIPES

BAKED APPLE

Ingredients

    1 medium apple
    1-1/2 teaspoon sugar
    1/8 teaspoon cinnamon
    1 2-1/2" square graham cracker
    1/4 cup water

Wash, peel and core apple. Cut in 1/4" slices. Put water and apple slices into small skillet and cook on medium heat for five minutes until tender. Drain any excess water from apples. Mix cinnamon and sugar together. Sprinkle over apples. Remove apples from pan. Crush graham crackers. Sprinkle over apple mixture.

Makes one serving

## VEGETABLE SOUP

Ingredients

    1/2 small green cabbage, cut into chunks
    1/2 green pepper, diced
    1 small onion
    2 (14 1/2 oz.) cans no-salt added whole, peeled
        tomatoes with juice
    3 stalks celery, diced

In a large saucepan toss all ingredients together. Bring to boil then simmer until vegetables are tender. Tastes great hot or cold.

Makes 4 to 5 one-cup servings

## GRILLED CHEESE SANDWICH

Ingredients

> 2 slices whole wheat bread
> 2 ounces diet cheese (55 calories or less per ounce)
> Pam cooking spray (or equivalent)

Spray small skillet with cooking spray. Spray one side of each slice of bread with cooking spray. Place one slice of bread on skillet, sprayed side down. Put cheese on bread slice. Top with second slice of bread, sprayed side up. Cook on medium heat until both sides are golden brown.

Makes one sandwich

## VEGETARIAN PITA (1000-CALORIE DIET)

Ingredients

> 1/2 pita bread
> 3/4 cup chopped lettuce
> 1/2 sliced tomato
> 1/4 cup sliced cucumber
> 1/4 cup bean sprouts
> 1 tbsp. Miracle Whip (fat free)
> 1 tsp. Grey Poupon Dijon Mustard

Mix dressing and mustard together. Set aside.

Toss lettuce, cucumber and tomato slices together. Add dressing and mustard mixture. Stuff mixture into pita bread. Top with bean sprouts.

Makes one serving.

## VEGETARIAN PITA (1200-CALORIE DIET)

Ingredients

1 pita bread (6" across)
1 cup chopped lettuce
1 tomato, sliced
1/2 cup sliced cucumbers
1/4 cup alfalfa sprouts
2 tbsp. fat-free dressing

Toss lettuce, cucumbers, tomato slices together. Add dressing. Stuff mixture into pita bread. Top with alfalfa sprouts.

Makes one serving.

## VEGETARIAN PITA (1500 CALORIE DIET)

Ingredients

> 1 pita bread (6" across)
> 1 cup chopped lettuce
> 1 tomato, sliced
> 1/2 cup sliced cucumbers
> 5 olives
> 1/4 cup diced green peppers
> 1/4 cup mushrooms
> 1/4 cup alfalfa sprouts
> 2 tbsp. fat-free dressing or 2 tbsp. Miracle Whip
> (fat free) and 2 tsp. dijon mustard

Toss lettuce, cucumbers, olives, green peppers, mushrooms, tomato slices together. Add dressing. Stuff mixture into pita bread. Top with alfalfa sprouts.

Makes one serving.

## STEAK FRIES

Ingredients

> 1 medium baking potato (washed)
> 1/4 teaspoon garlic powder
> 1/8 teaspoon paprika
> Pam cooking spray (or equivalent)

Preheat oven to 350 degrees. Spray baking sheet with Pam. Slice potato into 1/8" wedges. Place potato wedges on baking sheet so that they are not touching. Spray potatoes with Pam. Sprinkle garlic powder and paprika onto potato. Bake for 30 to 40 minutes. Turn once during cooking.

Makes one serving

## BAKED TORTILLA CHIPS

### Ingredients

1 package 7" soft tortilla shells
Non-stick cooking spray

Preheat oven to 325 degrees F. Spray both sides of tortilla shells with non-stick cooking spray. Cut tortilla shells into eight wedges. Spray baking sheet with non-stick spray. Place tortilla wedges on baking sheet and place in oven. Cook for six to eight minutes or until crisp. After cooling, chips can be stored in airtight container.

Eight chips = one serving

# REFERENCES

1. Lustig A, Weight loss programs: Failing to meet ethical standards? The Journal of American Dietetic Association. 1991; 91: 1253.

2. Wadden T, et al. Long-term Effects of Dieting on Resting Metabolic Rate in Obese Outpatients. JAMA, 1990; 264: 707–711.

3. Begley, CE, Government Should Strengthen Regulation in the Weight Loss Industry. 1991; 91: 1255.

4. Spielman A, et al. Cost of commercial weight loss programs found to vary widely. J. Am. Coll. Nutr, 92; 11: 36–41.

5. Blackburn GL, Improving the American Diet. American Journal of Public Health. 92; 82: 465.

6. Skelton N, Skelton III W, Medical Implications of Obesity. Post-graduate Medicine, 92; 92: 151–162.

7. Council on Scientific Affairs. Treatment of Obesity in Adults. JAMA, 88; 260: 2547.

8. Kuczmarski R, et al, Increasing Prevalence of Overweight Among US Adults. JAMA, 1994; 272: 205.

9. The University of Washington School of Medicine, Etiology of Obesity: Theoretical Perspectives. 1991; 2: 6.

10. Pi-Sunyer FX, The Fattening of America. JAMA, 1994; 272: 238–39.

11. Kramer FM, et al. Long-term follow up of behavioral treatment of obesity: patterns of regain among men and women. Int J Obes, 1989; 13: 123–126.

15. Wolfe G, Trozzolino L, Kern P, Exogenous Obesity: What actually works? Hospital Medicine, 93; 4: 112.

16. National Institute of Health Consumer Develop-

ment Conference Statements, Health Implication of Obesity. Annals of Internal Medicine, 1985; 103: 147–151.

17. Kingsley C, et al, How to reduce risk of coronary artery disease. Post-graduate Medicine, 92; 91: 147.

18. Itallie T, Health Implications of Overweight and Obesity in the United States. Ann Inter Med, 85; 103 (6 pt 2): 983–988.

19. Stephenson J, Risk Reduction Can Reverse Atherosclerosis. Family Practice News, 93; 23: 1.

20. Skerrett P, Primary-Care Doctors Are on the Front Lines of Stroke Prevention. Medical World News, 92; 2: 27.

21. Garbaciak Jr. J, et al, Maternal weight and pregnancy complications. Am J Obstet Gynecol, 85; 152: 238.

25. Lucas C, Excessive Weight Gain, Obesity lead to increased risk of gout. Obesity Update, 92; 2: 2.

27. Blackburn GL, Kanders, BS. Medical Evaluation and Treatment of Obese Patient. Am J Cardiol, 1987; 60: 55G–58G.

28. Ashley F, Kannel W. Relation of Weight Change to Changes in Atherogenic Traits: The Framingtem Study. J. Chronic Dis, 1974; 27: 103–114.

29. Fat Execs get Slimmer Paychecks. Industry Week, 1974; 180: 21–24.

30. Leveille GA, Adipose tissue metabolism: influence of periodicity of eating and diet composition. Fed Proc, 1970; 29: 1294–1301.

31. Bray, GA, Lipogenesis in human adipose tissue: some effects of nibbling and gorging. J Clin Invest, 1972; 51: 537–48.

32. Burton B, Fosler W, Itallie T, Health implication of obesity: NIH consensus development conference. International Journal of Obesity, 85; 9: 155–169.

# INDEX

# TEAR-OUT
# SHOPPING LISTS

# Week 1—1000 Calories

## Meats
- Chicken breast
- Tuna packed in water
- Ground sirloin
- Turkey breast
- Ham
- Flank steak
- Egg substitute
- Fish

## Fruits
- Cantaloupe
- Pineapple or canned pineapple chunks packed in water or own juice
- Pears
- Grapes
- Grapefruit
- Peaches or canned peaches packed in own juice or water
- Fruit cocktail packed in water or own juice
- Oranges

## Breads/starches
- Pancake mix (complete pancake mix or frozen pancakes with less than 2 grams of fat)
- Saltine crackers
- Potatoes
- Noodles
- Bran Flakes cereal
- Bagel
- Hamburger bun
- Whole wheat bread
- Pretzels
- Graham crackers
- Pita bread (6" across)
- White rice
- Popcorn
- Vanilla wafers
- Frozen soft pretzel

## Vegetables
- Canned tomatoes
- Green onion
- Cucumber
- Green pepper
- Broccoli
- Spinach
- Tomato juice
- Green beans
- Carrots
- Lettuce
- Tomato
- Celery
- Radishes
- Cauliflower
- Corn
- Peas

## Dairy products
- Skim milk
- Low-fat cottage cheese

Fat-free cheese
Non-fat frozen yogurt

Miscellaneous/
condiments
Diet jelly
Diet syrup

Pickles
Miracle Whip (fat free)
or fat-free margarine
Molly McButter
Fat-free cream cheese

# Week 2—1000 Calories

## Meats
Ham
Turkey breast
Tuna packed in water
Ground sirloin
Low-fat turkey lunch
  meat
Skinless chicken
  breast
Fish
Pork tenderloin
Egg substitute
Lean beef sirloin

## Fruits
Orange juice
Strawberries (If out of
  season substitute
  choice of canned
  fruit in water or own
  juice or frozen
  strawberries)
Cantaloupe
Apple
Plums (If out of season
  substitute choice of
  canned fruit in water
  or own juice)
Grapefruit
Grapes
Orange
Prunes or raisins
Pineapple chunks
packed in own juice
or water
Fruit cocktail packed
in own juice or
water

Blueberries (fresh or
frozen)

## Breads/starches
Bagels
Whole wheat bread
Popcorn
Bran Flakes
Pita Bread (6" across)
Saltine crackers
Hamburger bun
Potato
Vanilla wafers
Graham crackers
Noodles
Rice (white)
Pancake mix (complete
  pancake mix or
  frozen pancakes
  with less than 2
  grams of fat)

## Vegetables
Lettuce
Spinach
Green peppers
Alfalfa sprouts
Radishes

Peas
Corn
Carrots
Celery
Cauliflower
Cucumber
Canned tomatoes
Green onion
Broccoli
Mushrooms
Asparagus
Green beans

## Dairy products
Skim milk
Non-fat yogurt

Fat-free cheese
Non-fat frozen yogurt
Low-fat cottage cheese

## Miscellaneous/ condiments
Lemon juice
Pickles
Miracle Whip (fat free)
  or mayonnaise
Fat-free salad dressing
Sugar-free pudding
Sugar-free gelatin

# Week 3—1000 Calories

## Meats
- Egg substitute
- Healthy Choice hot dog
- Lean beef sirloin
- Tuna packed in water
- Skinless chicken
- Skinless turkey breast
- Fish
- Ham
- Pork tenderloin
- Shrimp

## Fruits
- Orange
- Peaches or canned peaches packed in own juice or water
- Bananas
- Prunes, raisins or plums
- Orange juice
- Apple
- Fruit cocktail packed in own juice or water
- Grapes
- Grapefruit
- Pineapple chunks packed in own juice or water

## Breads/starches
- Whole wheat bread
- Vanilla wafers
- Hot dog bun

- Potatoes
- Bran Flakes
- Bagel
- Rice
- Graham crackers
- Popcorn
- Grapenuts
- Pretzels
- Whole wheat crackers
- Pita bread (6″ across)
- Noodles
- Pancake mix (complete pancake mix or frozen pancakes with less than 2 grams of fat)

## Vegetables
- Sauerkraut
- Mushrooms
- Spinach
- Celery
- Lettuce
- Cucumber
- Beets
- Carrots
- Tomato
- Green beans
- Broccoli
- Tomato juice
- Brussels sprouts

Bean sprouts
Radishes

## Dairy products
Skim milk
Fat-free yogurt
Fat-free sour cream
Non-fat frozen yogurt
Low-fat cottage cheese
Parmesan cheese

## Miscellaneous condiments
Fat-free salad dressing

Pickles
Salsa
Mustard (Dijon)
Pickle relish
Sugar-free pudding
Miracle Whip (fat free)
  or mayonnaise
Diet jelly
Light syrup

## Week 4—1000 Calories

### Meats
Skinless chicken breast
Turkey
Tuna packed in water
Fish
Ham
Healthy Choice hot dog
Flank steak

### Fruits
Orange juice
Strawberries (if not in
season, substitute
choice of canned
fruit in own juice or
in water or frozen
strawberries)
Pineapple chunks in
own juice or water
Grapes
Banana
Cantaloupe
Pear
Apple

### Bread/Starches
Pancake mix (complete
pancake mix or
frozen pancakes
with less than 2
grams of fat)
Rice (white)
Pretzels
Whole wheat bread
Potatoes
Bagels
Rye-crisp crackers
English muffin
Pita bread
Popcorn
Graham crackers
Bran Flakes
Bread sticks
Noodles
Hot dog bun
Vanilla wafers

### Vegetables
Lettuce
Celery
Green onions
Carrots
Asparagus
Tomato juice
Broccoli
Zucchini
Bean sprouts
Mushrooms
Tomato
Canned tomatoes
Green beans
Cucumber
Green pepper
Brussels sprouts

### Dairy products
Skim milk
Low-fat cottage cheese

Fat-free yogurt
Fat-free cheese
Non-fat frozen yogurt

Miscellaneous/
condiments
Light syrup
Lemon juice

Diet pop
Sugar-free gelatin
Diet jelly
Salsa
Honey
Weight Watchers Smart
One Lemon Herb
Chicken

# Week 1—1200 Calories

## Meats
Egg substitute
Turkey breast
Shrimp
Pork tenderloin
Ground sirloin
Fish
Healthy Choice hot dog
Tuna packed in water
Ham
Beef tenderloin

## Fruits
Orange juice
Grapes
Pears
Plum
Grapefruit or grapefruit
    juice
Apples
Banana
Pineapple chunks
    packed in own juice
    or water
Fruit cocktail packed
    in own juice or
    water
Oranges
Strawberries, fresh or
    frozen
Fruit juice
Peach or canned
    peaches in own juice
    or water
Cantaloupe
Kiwi

## Breads/starches
Oatmeal
Whole wheat bread
Rice (white or brown)
Bagels
Whole-grain English
    muffins
Potatoes
Grapenuts
Bran Flakes
Pita bread (6" across)
Popcorn
Saltine crackers
Hamburger bun
Graham crackers
Pancake mix (complete
    pancake mix or
    frozen pancakes
    with less than 2
    grams of fat)
Hot dog bun
Noodles

## Vegetables
Lettuce
Mushrooms
Green pepper
Onion
Pea pods
Spinach
Tomato juice

Carrots
Celery
Tomato
Alfalfa sprouts
Cucumbers
Broccoli
Beets
Sauerkraut
Cauliflower
Green beans

Dairy
Skim milk
Non-fat yogurt
Margarine or diet
margarine

Fat-free cheese
Low-fat cottage cheese
Non-fat frozen yogurt

Miscellaneous/
condiments
Sunflower seeds
Fat-free salad dressing
Pickles
Miracle Whip (fat free)
or mayonnaise
Diet jam or jelly
Sugar-free gelatin
Diet syrup

# Week 2—1200 Calories

## Meats
- Turkey
- Chicken breast
- Ham
- Fish
- Tuna packed in water
- Healthy Choice hot dog

## Fruits
- Raisins
- Orange juice
- Watermelon (If out of season may substitute canned fruit in own juice or in water)
- Cantaloupe
- Apples
- Kiwi
- Nectarine
- Grapes
- Pear
- Oranges
- Peach or canned peaches in own juice or water
- Plums
- Grapefruit
- Strawberries, fresh or frozen
- Pineapple chunks packed in own juice or water
- Fruit cocktail packed in own juice or water
- Banana
- Prunes
- Apple juice

## Breads/starches
- Bran Flakes
- Whole wheat bread
- Rice (white or brown)

- Bagels
- Popcorn
- English muffins
- Graham crackers
- Potato
- Grapenuts
- Pancake mix (complete pancake mix or frozen pancakes with less than 2 grams of fat)
- Hot dog bun
- Saltine crackers
- Flour tortilla shells (7 inch)

## Vegetables
- Celery
- Cauliflower
- Broccoli
- Carrots
- Lettuce

Spinach
Radish
Mushrooms
Green beans
Tomato
Asparagus
Zucchini
Corn
Pimentos
Sauerkraut

## Dairy

Skim milk
Non-fat yogurt
Low-fat cottage cheese
Non-fat frozen yogurt
Fat-free cheese
Margarine or diet
    margarine

## Miscellaneous/condiments

Salsa
Miracle Whip (fat free)
    or mayonnaise
Fat-free salad dressing
Sugar-free pudding
Diet jam or jelly
Budget Light Oriental
    Beef frozen entree
Sugar-free gelatin
Budget Light Sirloin of
    Beef in Herb Sauce
    frozen entree
Diet syrup

# Week 3—1200 Calories

## Meats

- Tuna packed in water
- Turkey
- Ham
- Shrimp
- Ground sirloin hamburger
- Pork tenderloin
- Fish
- Egg substitute

## Fruits

- Raisins
- Cantaloupe
- Peaches or canned peaches in own juice or water
- Raspberries (If not in season may substitute canned fruit packed in own juice or water)
- Apple juice
- Plums
- Orange
- Fruit cocktail packed in own juice or water
- Orange juice
- Pear
- Blueberries, fresh or frozen
- Bananas
- Applesauce
- Fruit juice
- Prunes
- Strawberries, fresh or frozen
- Grapes
- Pineapple chunks packed in own juice or water
- Apple

## Breads/starches

- Bran Flakes
- Pita bread (6" across)
- Stuffing
- Popcorn
- Oatmeal
- Whole wheat bread
- Vanilla wafers
- Rice (white or brown)
- Whole-grain English muffin
- Pretzels
- Graham crackers
- Noodles
- Bagel
- Pancake mix (complete pancake mix or frozen pancakes with less than 2 grams of fat)
- Bread sticks
- Flour tortilla shells (7 inches)

## Vegetables

- Lettuce
- Celery
- Carrots
- Beets
- Brussels sprouts
- Broccoli
- Mixed vegetables
- Spinach
- Mushrooms
- Cucumber
- Tomato
- Alfalfa sprouts
- Water chestnuts
- Tomato juice
- Radishes
- Peas
- Cauliflower
- Green beans

## Dairy

- Skim milk
- Non-fat yogurt
- Fat-free shredded cheddar cheese
- Non-fat frozen yogurt
- Low-fat cottage cheese
- Margarine or diet margarine
- Fat-free cream cheese

## Miscellaneous/ condiments

- Fat-free salad dressing
- Diet jam or jelly
- Sugar-free gelatin
- Stouffer's Lean Cuisine Breast of Chicken Parmesan
- Diet syrup
- Salsa

# Week 4—1200 Calories

## Meats

- Ham
- Turkey
- Pork tenderloin
- Tuna
- Chicken breast
- Fish
- Beef tenderloin
- Egg substitute
- Healthy Choice hot dog
- Cornish hen

## Fruits

- Orange
- Pineapple chunks packed in own juice or water
- Pear
- Grapefruit or grapefruit juice
- Raisins
- Peaches or canned peaches in own juice or water
- Orange juice
- Grapes
- Banana
- Applesauce
- Plums
- Fruit cocktail packed in own juice or water
- Fruit juice
- Kiwi
- Strawberries, fresh or frozen
- Blueberries, fresh or frozen

## Breads/starches

- Bran Flakes
- Whole wheat bread
- Potatoes
- Popcorn
- Bagels
- Graham crackers
- Pita (6" across)
- Soft frozen pretzel
- English muffin
- Rice (white or brown)
- Vanilla wafers
- Bread sticks
- Pancake mix (complete pancake mix or frozen pancakes with less than 2 grams of fat)
- Hot dog buns

## Vegetables

- Lettuce
- Tomato
- Carrots
- Tomato juice
- Corn
- Broccoli
- Canned tomatoes

Green onions
Green pepper
Cucumber
Alfalfa sprouts
Peas
Celery
Zucchini
Mushrooms
Spinach
Beets
Cauliflower
Radish
Onion
Sauerkraut
Red cabbage
Water chestnuts
Green beans

## Dairy

Skim milk
Low-fat cottage cheese
Fat-free frozen yogurt
Fat-free cream cheese
Margarine or diet
    margarine

## Miscellaneous/ condiments

Weight Watchers Smart
    One Lasagna
    Florentine
Peanuts
Sugar-free gelatin
Miracle Whip (fat-free)
    or mayonnaise
Fat-free salad dressing
Diet syrup

# Week 1—1500 Calories

## Meats

- Tuna packed in water
- Ground sirloin hamburger
- Turkey breast
- Ham
- Skinless chicken breast
- Flank steak
- Fish
- Egg substitute

## Fruits

- Fruit cocktail in own juice or water
- Orange juice
- Plums
- Peaches or canned peaches in own juice or water
- Fruit juice
- Grapefruit
- Grapes
- Raisins
- Apple juice
- Cantaloupes
- Apple
- Watermelon (If not in season may substitute canned fruit in juice or water)
- Orange
- Pineapple chunks in own juice or water
- Plums

## Bread/starches

- Bran Flakes
- Whole wheat bread
- Pita bread
- Graham crackers
- Hamburger bun
- Potato
- Pretzels
- Vanilla wafers
- Rice (white or brown)
- Popcorn
- Bread sticks
- Saltine crackers
- Soft frozen pretzel
- Grapenuts
- Noodles

## Vegetables

- Tomato juice
- Green beans
- Carrots
- Celery
- Peas
- Beets
- Lettuce
- Cucumber
- Alfalfa sprouts
- Broccoli
- Mushrooms
- Tomato
- Radishes

Cauliflower
Corn
Spinach
Canned tomatoes
Green onion
Green pepper

Dairy

Skim milk
Fat-free yogurt
Non-fat frozen yogurt
Fat-free sour cream
Parmesan cheese
Fat-free cheese

Margarine or diet
margarine

Miscellaneous/
condiments

Miracle Whip (fat free)
or mayonnaise
Diet jam or jelly
Sunflower seeds
Molly McButter
Pickles
Fat-free dressing
Light syrup

# Week 2—1500 Calories

## Meats
- Ham
- Turkey
- Tuna packed in water
- Ground sirloin hamburger
- Skinless chicken breast
- Shrimp
- Pork tenderloin
- Egg substitute
- Beef sirloin steak

## Fruits
- Orange juice
- Raisins
- Strawberries, fresh or frozen
- Cantaloupe
- Apple
- Plums
- Nectarine
- Pears
- Grapefruit
- Fruit juice
- Grapes
- Orange
- Prunes
- Peaches or canned peaches in own juice or water
- Banana
- Blueberries, fresh or frozen

## Breads/starches
- Bran Flakes
- Bagels
- Whole wheat bread
- Rice (white or brown)
- Popcorn
- Pita bread
- Saltine crackers
- Hamburger bun
- Potato
- Vanilla wafers
- Graham crackers
- Noodles
- Grapenuts
- Pancake mix (complete pancake mix or frozen pancakes with less than 2 grams of fat)
- Frozen soft pretzel

## Vegetables
- Celery
- Green beans
- Lettuce
- Cauliflower
- Radishes
- Green onion
- Cucumber
- Carrots
- Tomatoes
- Canned tomatoes
- Green pepper

Green onion
Asparagus
Broccoli
Mushrooms
Brussels sprouts
Spinach
Peas
Corn

## Dairy

Skim milk
Margarine or diet
   margarine
Non-fat yogurt

Fat-free cream cheese
Non-fat frozen yogurt
Low-fat cottage cheese

## Miscellaneous/ condiments

Pickles
Miracle Whip (fat free)
   or mayonnaise
Fat-free dressing
Sugar-free pudding
Sugar-free gelatin
Light syrup

# Week 3—1500 Calories

## Meats
- Tuna packed in water
- Chicken
- Turkey
- Fish
- Ham
- Beef sirloin
- Pork tenderloin
- Shrimp
- Healthy Choice hot dogs

## Fruits
- Orange juice
- Prunes
- Fruit juice
- Orange
- Apple
- Pears
- Strawberries, fresh or frozen
- Banana
- Grapes
- Fruit cocktail in own juice or water
- Grapefruit
- Pineapple chunks in own juice or water
- Cantaloupe

## Breads/starches
- Bran Flakes
- Pita bread
- Rice (white or brown)
- Graham crackers
- Whole wheat bread

- Popcorn
- Bagel
- Grapenuts
- Bread sticks
- Potatoes
- Whole wheat crackers
- Frozen soft pretzel
- Noodles
- Vanilla wafers
- Pancake mix (complete pancake mix or frozen pancakes with less than 2 grams of fat)
- Saltine crackers
- Hot dog buns

## Vegetables
- Celery
- Spinach
- Cucumber
- Beets
- Carrots
- Tomatoes
- Green beans
- Corn
- Tomato juice
- Green peppers
- Cauliflower
- Squash
- Lettuce

Mushrooms
Broccoli
Brussels sprouts
Green pepper
Green onion
Canned tomatoes
Radishes
Sauerkraut

## Dairy

Skim milk
Non-fat yogurt
Margarine or diet
    margarine
Non-fat frozen yogurt

Low-fat cottage cheese
Fat-free cream cheese
Parmesan cheese

## Miscellaneous/ condiments

Miracle Whip (fat free)
    or mayonnaise
Fat-free dressing
Pickle relish
Dijon mustard
Sugar-free pudding
Light syrup

# Week 4—1500 Calories

## Meats

Turkey
Chicken
Egg substitute
Tuna packed in
water
Fish
Ham
Healthy Choice hot
dogs
Flank steak

## Fruits

Orange juice
Pineapple chunks in
own juice or water
Cantaloupe
Grapefruit or grapefruit
juice
Grapes
Apple
Banana
Prunes
Pears
Raisins
Orange
Plums
Fruit juice

## Breads/starches

Whole wheat bread
Potatoes
Bagel
Bread sticks
English muffins

Flour tortilla shells (7
inches)
Pita bread
Saltine crackers
Popcorn
Rice (white or brown)
Bran Flakes
Vanilla wafers
Hot dog buns
Noodles
Grapenuts
Pancake mix (complete
pancake mix or
frozen pancakes
with less than 2
grams of fat)
Frozen soft pretzel

## Vegetables

Celery
Tomato juice
Broccoli
Lettuce
Green onions
Zucchini
Bean sprouts
Tomatoes
Canned tomatoes
Green peppers
Cucumber
Carrots

Corn
Mushrooms
Spinach
Alfalfa sprouts
Green beans
Sauerkraut
Tomato juice
Asparagus

## Dairy

Margarine or diet
  margarine
Skim milk
Fat-free shredded
  cheddar cheese
Fat-free cream cheese
Low-fat cottage cheese

Fat-free yogurt
Non-fat frozen yogurt

## Miscellaneous/ condiments

Diet jelly or jam
Fat-free pudding
Lemon juice
Weight Watchers Smart
  One Lemon Herb
  Chicken
Salsa
Honey
Miracle Whip (fat free)
  or mayonnaise
Fat-free dressing
Fig Newtons
Light syrup

## Week 1—1800 Calories

### Meats

Turkey breast
Shrimp
Pork tenderloin
Egg substitute
Tuna packed in water
Ham
Ground round
   hamburger
Chicken
Healthy Choice hot
   dogs
Fish
Beef tenderloin

### Fruits

Oranges
Pears
Raisins
Grapefruit or grapefruit
   juice
Apple
Banana
Pineapple juice in own
   juice or water
Fruit cocktail in own
   juice or water
Peach or canned
   peaches in own juice
   or water
Cantaloupe
Blueberries (fresh or
   frozen)

### Breads

Whole wheat bread
Oatmeal
Rice (white or brown)
Pretzels
Bagels
Wheat grain English
   muffins
Graham crackers
Potatoes
Grapenuts
Bran Flakes
Pita bread
Dinner roll
Saltine crackers
Hamburger bun
Stuffing
Pancake mix (complete
   pancake mix or
   frozen pancakes
   with less than 2
   grams of fat)
Hot dog buns
Noodles
Fig Newtons
Wheat crackers
Bread sticks (crisp)

### Vegetables

Carrots
Lettuce
Mushrooms
Onion

Green pepper
Spinach
Peapods
Cauliflower
Tomato juice
Celery
Tomato
Bean sprouts
Broccoli
Alfalfa sprouts
Cucumbers
Beets
Sauerkraut
Peas
Radish
Green beans

## Dairy
Margarine
Skim milk
Fat-free cream cheese

Low-fat cheese
Non-fat yogurt
Low-fat cottage cheese
Low-fat frozen yogurt

## Miscellaneous/ condiments
Fat-free dressing
Almonds
Peanuts
Pickles
Miracle Whip (fat free)
Weight Watchers
    Lemon Herb Chicken
    Riccata
Sugar-free gelatin
Diet syrup
Natural peanut butter

# Week 2—1800 Calories

## Meats
- Turkey
- Chicken
- Ham
- Tuna packed in water
- Fish
- Healthy Choice hot dogs

## Fruits
- Raisins
- Apricots
- Oranges
- Apples
- Cantaloupe
- Peach or canned peaches in own juice or water
- Fruit juice
- Orange juice
- Grapes
- Pear
- Pineapple chunks in own juice or water
- Bananas
- Plums
- Fruit juice
- Grapefruit or grapefruit juice
- Strawberries, fresh or frozen
- Applesauce

## Breads/starches
- Whole wheat bread
- Bran Flakes
- Noodles
- Grapenuts

- Oatmeal
- Bread sticks (crisp)
- Bagels
- Dinner rolls
- Popcorn
- English muffins
- Pretzels
- Graham crackers
- Low-fat granola bar
- Vanilla wafers
- Saltine crackers
- Fig Newtons
- Potatoes
- Flour tortilla shells (7 inches)
- Pancakes (complete pancake mix or frozen pancakes with less than 2 grams of fat)
- Hot dog buns
- Rice (white or brown)
- Frozen soft pretzel

## Vegetables
- Celery
- Tomatoes

Lettuce
Broccoli
Corn
Carrots
Cauliflower
Water chestnuts
Zucchini
Spinach
Green peppers
Cucumber
Mushrooms
Beets
Green beans
Brussels sprouts
Red cabbage
Radishes
Asparagus

Dairy
Skim milk
Fat-free yogurt

Fat-free cheese
Margarine
Low-fat cottage cheese
Low-fat frozen yogurt

Miscellaneous/
condiments
Diet jam or jelly
Miracle Whip (fat free)
Sugar-free pudding
Fat-free dressing
Budget Light Oriental
Beef frozen entree
Bean soup
Salsa
Budget Gourmet Light
Sirloin of Beef in
Herb Sauce

## Week 3—1800 Calories

### Meats

Tuna packed in water
Turkey
Shrimp
Ham
Ground round
Chicken
Pork tenderloin
Eggs
Fish

### Fruits

Raisins
Fruit juice
Peaches or canned
    peaches in own juice
    or water
Raspberries (If not in
    season may
    substitute canned
    fruit in own juice or
    water)
Apple juice
Plums
Orange
Fruit cocktail in own
    juice or water
Orange juice
Grapes
Pear
Blueberries, fresh or
    frozen
Watermelon (If not in
season may
substitute canned
fruit in own juice or
water)
Cantaloupe
Applesauce
Prunes
Strawberries, fresh or
    frozen
Pineapple chucks in
    own juice or water
Orange juice
Banana

### Breads

Bran Flakes
Whole wheat bread
Pita bread
Stuffing
Popcorn
Noodles
Oatmeal
Vanilla wafers
Whole wheat English
    muffins
Pretzels
Corn muffin
Tortilla Shells
Low-fat crackers
Rice (white or brown)
Dinner roll
Pancakes (complete
    pancake mix or
    frozen pancakes

with less than 2
grams of fat)
Muffin
Grapenuts
Garlic bread
Flour tortilla shells (7
inches)
Bread sticks (crisp)

Vegetables
Lettuce
Carrot
Celery
Squash
Brussels sprouts
Broccoli
Mixed vegetables
Cucumbers
Tomatoes
Green onion
Alfalfa sprouts
Spinach
Tomato juice
Peas
Radish
Mushrooms
Cauliflower

Dairy
Skim milk
Non-fat yogurt
Fat-free frozen yogurt
Fat-free cream cheese
Margarine
Low-fat cottage cheese
Fat-free cheese

Miscellaneous/
condiments
Miracle Whip (fat free)
Fat-free refried beans
Salsa
Sugar-free gelatin
Diet jam or jelly
Fat-free dressing
Peanut butter
Stouffer's Lean Cuisine
Breast of Chicken
Parmesan
Sugar-free pudding
Diet syrup

## Week 4—1800 Calories

### Meats

- Ham
- Turkey
- Chicken
- Pork tenderloin
- Tuna packed in water
- Fish
- Eggs
- Beef tenderloin
- Healthy Choice hot dog
- Cornish hen

### Fruits

- Orange
- Pineapple chunks in own juice or water
- Pears
- Fruit juice
- Peaches or canned peaches in own juice or water
- Orange juice
- Apples
- Raisins
- Grapes
- Plums
- Fruit cocktail in own juice or water
- Applesauce
- Grapefruit or grapefruit juice
- Banana
- Blueberries (fresh or frozen)

### Breads

- Bran Flakes
- Whole wheat bread
- Pretzels
- Bread sticks (crisp)
- Dinner roll
- Popcorn
- Bagel
- Graham crackers
- Saltine crackers
- Garlic bread
- Pita bread
- Potatoes
- Noodles
- English muffin
- Muffin
- Vanilla wafers
- Rice (white or brown)
- Low-fat crackers
- Pancakes (complete pancake mix or frozen pancakes with less than 2 grams of fat)
- Grapenuts
- Hot dog buns

### Vegetables

- Lettuce
- Tomatoes
- Tomato juice
- Corn

Broccoli
Cucumbers
Green pepper
Green onion
Canned tomatoes
Beets
Peas
Carrots
Celery
Mushrooms
Radish
Cauliflower
Sauerkraut
Green beans

## Dairy

Low-fat cheese
Skim milk
Margarine
Non-fat frozen yogurt

Fat-free cream cheese
Egg
Fat-free yogurt
Low-fat cottage cheese

## Miscellaneous/ condiments

Diet jam or jelly
Weight Watchers Smart
    One Lasagna
    Florentine
Sugar-free gelatin
Dijon mustard
Low-fat granola bars
Fig Newtons
Miracle Whip (fat free)
Fat-free salad dressing
Peanut butter
Sugar-free pudding

SUPER SAVINGS OF $10.00
WHEN YOU PURCHASE BOTH OF DR. KAURA'S HIGHLY
ACCLAIMED BOOKS:

## *A Family Doctor's Guide to Understanding & Preventing Cancer* and *The Nibbler's Diet*™
by S.R. Kaura MD and Diane Collins, RD
For Only $34.95

Name _____

Address _____

City, State, Zip _____

Phone ( )_____

M/C _____ Visa_____ Disc_____ Amerex _____

# _____ Exp Date _____

Please Add $4.00 For Shipping & Handling
For Faster Service Call
Manisha Press
1-800-382-1190

SUPER SAVINGS OF $5.00
WHEN YOU BUY DR. KAURA'S HIGHLY ACCLAIMED:

## *A Family Doctor's Guide to Understanding & Preventing Cancer*
For Only $19.95

Name _____

Address _____

City, State, Zip _____

Phone ( )_____

M/C _____ Visa_____ Disc_____ Amerex _____

# _____ Exp Date _____

Please Add $4.00 For Shipping & Handling
For Faster Service Call
Manisha Press
1-800-382-1190